Colorful Crochet

With More Than 20 New Crochet Projects

Marianne Dekkers-Roos

TUVA

Tuva Publishing
www.tuvapublishing.com

Address Merkez Mah. Cavusbasi Cad. No:71
Cekmekoy - Istanbul 34782 / Turkey
Tel: +9 0216 642 62 62

Colorful Crochet

First Print 2017 / May

All Global Copyrights Belong To
Tuva Tekstil ve Yayıncılık Ltd

Content Crochet

Editor in Chief Ayhan DEMİRPEHLİVAN
Project Editor Kader DEMİRPEHLİVAN
Designer & Author Marianne DEKKERS-ROOS
Technical Editors Wendi CUSINS, Leyla ARAS, Büşra ESER
Graphic Design Ömer ALP, Abdullah BAYRAKÇI
Assistant Zilal ÖNEL

Photography Marianne Dekkers-Roos, Quinn Dekkers,
Carter Dekkers, Janneke Assink, Lisanne Multem and Tuva Publishing

ISBN 978-605-5647-97-1

Printing House
Bilnet Matbaacılık ve Ambalaj San A.Ş.

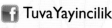

 TuvaYayincilik TuvaPublishing
 TuvaYayincilik TuvaPublishing

Contents

Introduction

For as long as I remember I've been creative. As a child I liked to draw, color, paint, make puppets, decorate little boxes with the shells I found on the beach - anything crafty, I loved it! I can't thank my expert sock-knitting grandmother, Marie, and my "let's-do-it-all" creative mother, Lien, enough for being my inspiring role-models, and for teaching me a lot of basic craft skills early on.

When my husband's career took us to the USA for eight years in the early 1990s, and my own professional career came to a halt, it was great fun to rekindle my creative side. Sewing, quilting, cross-stitching, knitting, decorative painting: I simply tried everything!

In 2010, I finally rediscovered crochet, after a lull of some forty years. There was nothing awkward about holding a hook and some yarn in my hands again after so long. For me, crochet was definitely "once learned, never forgotten". Almost immediately I became aware of a difference compared to the other crafts I was trying out. Crochet very rapidly became my favorite and absolute Number One craft - and it still is.

I quickly found out how much I liked playing with stitches and colors, and started putting my own little twists on existing crochet patterns. Beginning a blog at the end of 2013 seemed like a natural step in this process - a step that I loved taking too. The wonderful response to my work was all the encouragement I needed to start designing. Knowing that people are inspired by the things I make, that they crochet and enjoy the patterns that I come up with, is a fabulous and gratifying feeling.

You'll notice that one of the projects in this book is a copy of my very first crochet project, the project that taught me how to crochet. It's a poncho in pink, green, and off-white, which I first made when I was only nine years old.

I'm a bit sentimental about this poncho, and am delighted that it's part of my book. You see, this project was the start of a tremendous amount of crochet pleasure and achievement I experienced much later in life. Crochet has not only brought me joy, satisfaction, peace of mind (and more crochet projects than my studio can hold), but also a wealth of other wonderful side effects.

In fact, crochet was the seed that eventually led to my blog, to the many fantastic crafty friendships (lovely virtual ones all around the world, as well as in-person ones), and now to this book. I hope "Colorful Crochet" will inspire you to do what makes me happy - crochet – and bring you the same sense of joy while doing so!

Love,

Marianne xx

Amstelveen, May 2017

Before You Begin

Things I Learned (the Hard Way)

Diving head-first into a project before reading and understanding the pattern, never turned out well for me. I've learned to take the time to read through everything first, making sure I have all the yarn and notions needed to complete the project. Also, if there are stitches or techniques I am unfamiliar with, I practice these before starting (these stitch sample swatches are great to keep as a reference; or you could sew them all together to make a 'scrap' blanket).

Another hint before beginning a new project, is to crochet a 4" (10 cm) square swatch, in the pattern stitches used in the project. Try using different hook sizes (or even different yarn weights) to get the right 'feel' of the fabric (either firm or loose – depending on the project). Doing this swatch is important, especially when you want to alter the finished size of the pattern. From this swatch, you can determine how many stitches and rows you will need for your new project.

Everyone dislikes weaving in ends, but I strongly believe it's worth the extra effort to do a good job here. There's nothing worse than putting hours of love into a project, only to have the stitches fall apart because you just cut off your ends. Or worse still, have your magic ring disintegrate!

When beginning and ending, leave a decent length long end for sewing in. Then use a yarn needle and on the wrong side of the project weave the yarn end through a few stitches one way and then another, then across and back again, making sure it's firmly woven in and not visible from the right side.

When you know that you are going to be sewing crocheted pieces together, leaving a long end (or starting with a long end) comes in really handy. You then use this long end and a yarn needle to sew the pieces together.

In this great day of modern technology, whenever I'm a bit unclear on certain crochet stitches or techniques, the internet comes to my rescue. I'm a 'visual' person and pick up things easier when watching someone else demonstrate. There are so many different crochet channels to watch, so if one video is unclear on the technique, watch someone else demonstrate it.

Happy crocheting!

Marianne

SKILL LEVEL SYMBOLS & DESCRIPTION

*	Easy	Project uses basic stitches, repetitive stitch patterns, simple color changes, and simple shaping and finishing
**	Intermediate	Project uses a variety of more advanced techniques, including color patterns, mid-level shaping and finishing
***	Challenging	Project has stitch patterns, techniques and dimension, such as non-repeating patterns, multi-color techniques, detailed shaping and refined finishing

HOOK SIZES TABLE

Millimeter Range	U.S. Size Range
2.25 mm	B-1
2.75 mm	C-2
3.25 mm	D-3
3.5 mm	E-4
3.75 mm	F-5
4 mm	G-6
4.5 mm	7
5 mm	H-8
5.5 mm	I-9
6 mm	J-10
6.5 mm	K-10 ½
8 mm	L-11
9 mm	M/N-13
10 mm	N/P-15
15 mm	P/Q
16 mm	Q
19 mm	S

YARNS USED IN DESIGNS

 DMC Natura Just Cotton

 DMC Woolly

 DMC Natura Just Cotton Medium

 DMC Natura Just Cotton XL

ABBREVIATIONS OF THE BASIC STITCHES

ch	Chain Stitch
sl st	Slip Stitch
sc	Single Crochet Stitch
hdc	Half-Double Crochet Stitch
dc	Double Crochet Stitch
tr	Treble (or Triple) Crochet Stitch

CONCISE ACTION TERMS

dec	Decrease (reduce by one or more stitches)
inc	Increase (add one or more stitches)
join	Join two stitches together, usually with a slip stitch. (Either to complete the end of a round or when introducing a new ball or color of yarn)
rep	Repeat (the previous marked instructions)
turn	Turn your crochet piece so you can work back for the next row/round
yo	Yarn over the hook. (Either to pull up a loop or to draw through the loops on hook)

STANDARD SYMBOLS USED IN PATTERNS

[ ]	Work instructions within brackets as many times as directed
( )	Work instructions within parentheses in same stitch or space indicated
*	Repeat the instructions following the single asterisk as directed
**	1) Repeat instructions between asterisks as many times as directed; or 2) Repeat from a given set of instructions
♥ ♥ ♥	Repeat instructions between hearts as many times as directed

CROCHET TERMINOLOGY

This book is written using US crochet terminology.

Here is a basic conversion chart:

US	UK
slip stitch **(sl st)**	slip stitch **(sl st)**
chain **(ch)**	chain **(ch)**
single crochet **(sc)**	double crochet **(dc)**
double crochet **(dc)**	treble crochet **(tr)**
half-double crochet **(hdc)**	half treble **(htr)**
treble (triple) crochet **(tr)**	double treble **(dtr)**

US Crochet Terms		UK Crochet Terms	
⬭	Chain	⬭	Chain
•	Slip Stitch	•	Slip Stitch
+	Single Crochet	+	Double Crochet
⊤	Half-Double Crochet	⊤	Half-Treble Crochet
†	Double Crochet	†	Treble Crochet
‡	Treble Crochet	‡	Double Treble Crochet
‡	Double Treble	‡	Triple Treble
🝆	Double Crochet Bobble	🝆	Treble Crochet Bobble
◯	Magic Ring	◯	Magic Ring

Projects

Circle Bags & Wall Hanging

Skill Level
** / ***

eeeeeeeeeeeeeeeeeeeee

One of the (many) reasons why I love crochet as much as I do, is its versatility. Not only can one pattern give you a totally new-looking project when done in different colors, but changing to a different kind of yarn and hook size even takes "new-looking" to a whole other level. Originally written to create a large bag, this pattern turned out equally lovely in smaller sizes or as a doily/wall hanging: win-win!

eeeeeeeeeeeeeeeeeeeee

Finished Sizes

Large Bags
16 ½" (42 cm) diameter

Medium Bag
12" (31 cm) diameter

Small Bag/Wall Hanging
8" (21 cm) diameter

WHAT YOU'LL NEED

For All Bags

Yarn needle
Fabric for lining
Heavy duty fusible interfacing

Large Size Bags

✳ **DMC Natura Just Cotton XL**
For the bag in neutral colors
Main Color - MC (#32) - 3 balls
Contrasting Color - CC (#11) – 3 balls

For the colorful bag
Color A (#43) – 2 balls
Color B (#06) – 1 ball
Color C (#41) – 1 ball
Color D (#73) – 1 ball
Color E (#111) – 1 ball
Color F (#10) – 1 ball
Color G (#9) – 1 ball
Color H (#83) – 1 ball

Hook: Size L-11 (8 mm)

Set of leather bag handles

Medium Size Bag

✳ **DMC Natura Just Cotton Medium**
Color A (#444) - 2 balls
Color B (#126) - 1 ball
Color C (#44) - 1 ball
Color D (#77) - 1 ball
Color E (#41) - 1 ball
Color F (#109) - 1 ball
Color G (#09) - 1 ball
Color H (#198) - 1 ball

Hook: Size H-8 (5 mm)

Small Size Bag

✳ **DMC Natura Just Cotton**
Color A (N61) – 1 ball
Color B (N59) – 1 ball
Color C (N32) – 1 ball
Color D (N41) – 1 ball
Color E (N47) – 1 ball
Color F (N85) – 1 ball
Color G (N13) – 1 ball
Color H (N05) – 1 ball

Hook: Size E-4 (3.5 mm)

Wall Hanging
✳ **DMC Natura Just Cotton**
Main Color - MC (N26) - 1 ball

Hook: Size E-4 (3.5 mm)

Yarn Needle
Metal Ring - 8" (20 cm) diameter
Needle and matching thread

PATTERN NOTES

✳ Do not turn after each round
✳ Fasten off after each color change
✳ Weave in all ends as you go

For the colorful bags, please refer to the photos for the color changes
✳ Rounds 1, 5 and 12 are worked in Color A
✳ Rounds 3, 10 and 11 are worked in Color C

The pattern is written for the Large Size Bag made in neutral colors.

When starting a new color, join with the right side of the circle facing you.

For the wall hanging, there is no color change.

SPECIAL STITCHES

Bobble Stitch (bob): Yarn over hook, insert hook in next st or sp indicated and pull up a loop, yarn over and draw through 2 loops on hook (2 loops on hook). Yarn over and insert hook in same stich and pull up a loop (four loops on hook), yarn over draw through 2 loops on hook (3 loops remain), yarn over, draw through remaining 3 loops (bobble made).

Popcorn (pc): Work 4 dc in st or sp indicated, drop loop from hook, insert hook from front to back through first dc (of 4-dc group), place dropped loop on hook and pull through st (popcorn made).

Cluster (dc3tog): *Yarn over hook, insert hook in next st or sp indicated and pull up a loop, yarn over and draw through 2 loops on hook* (2 loops on hook), rep from * to ** twice (4 loops on hook), yarn over, draw through all 4 loops (cluster made).

Long Treble (long-tr): Yarn over hook twice, working in the specified round, insert hook in stitch or space indicated (from front to back through the fabric) and draw up a loop to the height of the current round (4 loops on hook), [yarn over and pull yarn through 2 loops on hook] three times.

Long Double Crochet (long-dc): Yarn over hook, working in specified round, insert hook in stitch or space indicated (from front to back through the fabric) draw up a loop to the height of the current round (3 loops on hook), [yarn over and pull yarn through 2 loops on hook] twice.

Long Stitches are worked in a row or round below the current row.

CIRCLE
Make 2 for each Bag/Make 1 for Wall Hanging

ROUND 1: (Right Side) With MC, ch 4, join with sl st to first ch to form a ring (*or start with a Magic Ring - see Techniques*), ch 4 (counts as first dc & ch-1, now and throughout), *dc in ring, ch 1; rep from * 10 times more; join with sl st to first dc (3rd ch of beg ch-4). (12 dc & 12 ch-1 sps)

ROUND 2: Sl st in first ch-1 sp, ch 2, dc in same sp (first bobble stitch made), ch 2, *bob (see Special Stitches) in next ch-1 sp, ch 2; rep from * around; join with sl st to first dc (NOT in beg ch-2). (12 bobbles, 12 ch-2 sps) Fasten off Color MC.

ROUND 3: With right side facing, join CC with sl st to any ch-2 sp, ch 5 (counts as first dc & ch-2, now and throughout), dc in same sp, *(dc, ch 2, dc) in next ch-2 sp; rep from * around; join with sl st to first dc (3rd ch of beg ch-5). (24 dc & 12 ch-2 sps)

ROUND 4: Sl st in next ch-2 sp, ch 3 (counts as first dc, now and throughout), 3 dc in same sp, drop lp from hook, insert hook from front to back through 3rd ch (of beg ch-3), place dropped lp on hook and pull through st (first pc made), ch 4, * pc (see Special Stitches) in next ch-2 sp, ch 4; rep from * around; join with sl st to top of first pc. (12 popcorns & 12 ch-4 sps)

Designer's Note: *Any looseness is taken care of in the following rounds.*

ROUND 5: Sl st in next ch-4 sp, ch 3 (counts as first dc now and troughout), 4 dc in same sp, *5 dc in next ch-4 sp; rep from * around; join with sl st to first dc (3rd ch of beg ch-3. (60 dc) Fasten off CC.

ROUND 6: With right side facing, join MC with sl st to 5th dc of any 5-dc group, ch 7 (counts as first dc & ch-4, now and throughout), dc in next dc (first dc of next 5-dc group), dc3tog (using each of next 3 dc – see Special Stitches), *dc in next dc, ch 4, dc in next dc, using each of the next 3 dc dc3tog; rep from * around; join with sl st to first dc (3rd ch of beg ch-7). (12 clusters, 24 dc & 12 ch-4 lps)

ROUND 7: Sl st in next ch-4 sp, ch 2 (does NOT count as first hdc), 5 hdc in same sp, hdc in each of next 3 dc, *5 hdc in next ch-4 sp, hdc in each of next 3 dc; rep from * around; join with sl st to first hdc. (96 hdc) Fasten off MC.

ROUND 8: With right side facing, join CC with sl st to third loop (see Techniques) of center hdc of any 5-hdc group, ch 2 (does NOT count as first hdc), working in the third loops only, 2 hdc in same hdc, hdc in each of next 7 hdc, *2 hdc in next hdc, hdc in each of next 7 hdc; rep from * around; join with sl st to first hdc. (108 hdc) Fasten off CC.

ROUND 9: With right side facing, join MC with sl st to sp between the sts of any 2-hdc group, ch 3 (counts as 1st dc now and throughout), 4 dc in same sp, ch 2, skip next 4 hdc, working in Rnd 7, long-tr (see Special Stitches) in sp before center hdc (of the single 3-hdc sts), ch 2, working in Rnd 8, skip next 4 hdc, *5 dc in sp between next 2-dc group, ch 2, skip next 4 hdc, working in Rnd 7, long-tr in sp before center hdc, ch 2, working in Rnd 8, skip next 4 hdc; rep from * around; join with sl st to first dc (3rd ch of beg ch-3). (12 shells, 12 long-tr & 24 ch-2 sps) Fasten off MC.

ROUND 10: With right side facing, using CC, join with sc (see Techniques) to center dc of any 5-dc shell, *ch 3, working over ch-sts into Rnd 8, from base of shell on Rnd 8, skip next 3 hdc, long-dc (see Special Stitches) in next hdc (before long-tr), ch 2, skip next hdc, long-dc in next hdc (after long-tr), ch 3**, working in Row 9, sc in center dc of next 5-dc group; rep from * around, ending at ** on final repeat; join with sl st to first sc. (12 sc, 24 long-dc, 24 ch-3 sps & 12 ch-2 sps)

ROUND 11: (For Bags Only) Ch 3, *3 dc in next ch-3 sp, dc in next dc, 2 dc in next ch-2 sp, dc in next dc, 3 dc in next ch-3 sp**, dc in next sc; rep from * around, ending at ** on final repeat; join with sl st to first dc. (120 dc) Fasten off CC. Continue with Round 12.

ROUND 11: (For Wall Hanging Only) Ch 1, sc in same st as joining, *3 sc in next ch-3 sp, sc in next dc, 2 sc in next ch-2 sp, sc in next dc, 3 sc in next ch-3 sp**, sc in next sc; rep from * around, ending at ** on final repeat; join with sl st to first sc. (120 sc) Fasten off. Continue with Wall Hanging Assembly.

ROUND 12: (For Bags Only) With right side facing, join MC with sl st to third loop behind any dc, ch 3, working only in the third loops, dc in each dc around; join with sl st to first dc. (120 dc) Fasten off MC. For the Bags, repeat Rounds 1-12 for second side.

GUSSET STRIP– Large Bag Only

ROW 1: (Right Side) Using MC, ch 96, working in the back ridge (see Techniques) of ch-sts, sc in 2nd ch from hook, *sc in next ch; rep from * across. (95 sc)

ROWS 2-5: Ch 1, turn, sc in each sc across. (95 sc) At the end of Row 5, DO NOT FASTEN OFF. Set aside.

MAKING THE LININGS (for all the Bags)

For all bags, using the size of the finished circle piece, trace out four fabric circles, adding a seam allowance.

For the large bag's gusset strip, cut two strips of fabric to the same size as the gusset strip, adding a seam allowance.

Designer's Tip: *Before sewing the linings, iron on heavy duty fusible interfacing onto the wrong side of two of the fabric circles, as well as on one of the fabric gusset strips (for the large bag). This makes the lining more stable.*

With wrong sides facing (right sides together), machine sew two of the fabric circles together, leaving a small opening. Repeat with the other two circles.

For the large bag, repeat sewing around the gusset strip, leaving the one short end open.

Turn all pieces inside out and hand stitch the openings closed.

ATTACHING GUSSET STRIP – LARGE BAGS ONLY

Pick up set aside loop on Gusset Strip, ch 1, turn. Hold the Gusset Strip behind one circular piece - right sides are facing (wrong sides are together).

Working through both pieces at the same time, sc through any stitch on last round of circular piece into first st of Gusset Strip, using only the top loops of the stitches (back loop from circular piece together with front loop from Gusset Strip), [sc in next st] across to end of Gusset Strip (first side attached).

Working in the Gusset Strip only, sc in each row across short end (5 sc).

Align the second circular piece in front of the other long side of Gusset Strip, working through both pieces together, sc in each (again: back and front loops only) st across to other end of Gusset Strip.

Work 5 more sc across the other short end of Gusset Strip. Join with sl st to the first sc made and fasten off.

ASSEMBLY OF LARGE BAGS

Using the finished lining pieces, hand stitch each long side of the fabric gusset strip to the circles.

Insert the lining into the Bag and hand stitch around the top, securing the lining to the bag.

Attach leather handles to either side of the bag

ASSEMBLY OF MEDIUM & SMALL BAGS

Holding both circular pieces with right sides facing (wrong sides together), working through both pieces at the same time, using only the top loops of the stitches (back loop of front circular piece and front loop from back circular piece), with Color A, join with sc to any st, matching stitches, sc in each of next 94 sts. Fasten off.

Sew the two finished lining circles together, leaving the opening the same width as the bag. Insert the lining into the bag and hand stitch around the top, securing the lining to the bag.

HANDLES (Make 2)

Medium Bag

ROW 1: (Right Side) Using Color A, ch 86, working in back ridges of ch-sts, dc in 4th ch from hook (skipped ch-3 counts as first dc), *dc in next ch; rep from * across. (84 dc) Fasten off.

With right side facing, using color C, surface stitch (see Techniques) across top and bottom of handle. Repeat on second handle.

Using yarn needle, sew a handle to either side of bag.

Small Bag

Measure off two pieces of thin cord (or Natura XL) 32" (80 cm) long. Work sc stitches over each length of the cord. Fasten off.

Using yarn needle, sew a handle to either side of bag.

ASSEMBLY OF WALL HANGING

Using MC, with slip knot on hook, insert hook into metal ring, yo and pull up a loop, yo and draw through both loops on hook (first sc made), continue working single crochet stitches around metal ring to cover. Join with sl st to first sc. Fasten off.

Position the circular piece inside the covered ring. Using the needle and matching thread evenly sew the last round of the circular piece to the sc-sts at the back of the ring. Fasten off.

Using MC, make a hanger by chaining about 50 sts. Fasten off. Attach the hanger to the ring.

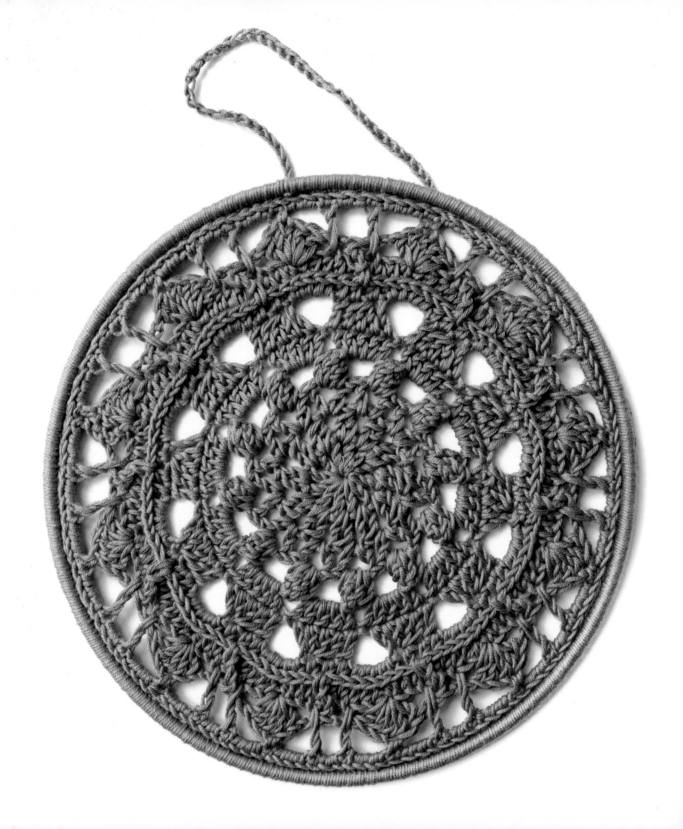

20

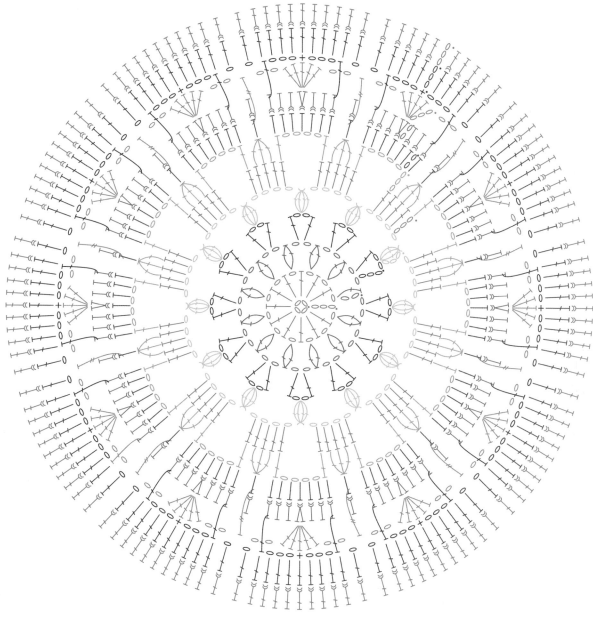

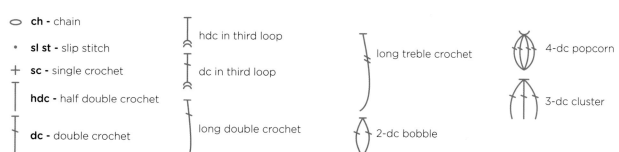

○ **ch -** chain

• **sl st -** slip stitch

+ **sc -** single crochet

| **hdc -** half double crochet

⊤ **dc -** double crochet

hdc in third loop

dc in third loop

long double crochet

long treble crochet

2-dc bobble

4-dc popcorn

3-dc cluster

Boho Cushion

Skill Level
**

The very first project I made using the Boho Triangle was the Boho Vest. The saying "the more creativity you use, the more you have" was definitely applicable here. While I was working on the vest the idea of the triangle used in a round cushion was born. Since the pattern for the cushion is definitely less of a challenge than the vest, it's a good idea to make the cushion first. This way you're easing yourself into the triangle-making, and can even practice the join-as-you-go method if you want to. Crocheted with the beautiful DMC Natura XL and a bigger hook, you only need six motifs to create your very own.

Finished Size

To fit a 20" (50 cm)
round pillow form

WHAT YOU'LL NEED

✱ **DMC Natura Just Cotton XL**
Blue (#73) – 3 balls

Hooks:
Size L-11 (8 mm) – for Triangles
Size K 10 ½ - (6.5 mm) – for border

Yarn Needle
Round Pillow Form - 20″ (50 cm) diameter

Fabric to cover pillow form

Needle and matching thread

PATTERN NOTES

✱ Do not turn after each round
✱ Weave in all ends as you go

SPECIAL STITCHES

Popcorn (pc): Work 3 dc in st or sp indicated, drop loop from hook, insert hook from front to back through first dc (of 3-dc group), place dropped loop on hook and pull through st (popcorn made).

TRIANGLE – Make 6

ROUND 1: (Right Side) Using the larger hook, ch 5, join with sl st to first ch to form a ring (or start with a Magic Ring - see Techniques); ch 4 (counts as first dc & ch-1, now and throughout), (dc, ch 1, dc, ch 2, tr, ch 2) in ring, *(dc, [ch 1, dc] twice, ch 2, tr, ch 2) in ring; rep from * once more; join with sl st to first dc (3rd ch of beg ch-4). (9 dc, 3 tr, 6 ch-1 sps & 6 ch-2 sps)

ROUND 2: Ch 1, sc in same st as joining, *[sc in next ch-1 sp, sc in next dc] twice, ch 2, pc (see Special Stitches) in next ch-2 sp, ch 3, sc in next tr, ch 3, pc in next ch-2 sp, ch 2**, sc in next dc; rep from * around, ending at ** on final rep; join with sl st to first sc. (18 sc, 6 popcorns, 6 ch-2 sps, 6 ch-3 sps)

ROUND 3: Ch 3 (counts as first dc, now and throughout), *dc in each of next 4 sc, skip ch-2 sp, sc in top of next pc, skip ch-3 sp, (3 tr, ch 2, dtr, ch 2, 3 tr) in next sc, skip ch-3 sp, sc in top of next pc, skip ch-2 sp**, dc in next sc; rep from * around, ending at ** on final rep; join with sl st to first dc (3rd ch of beg ch-3). (15 dc, 6 sc, 18 tr, 3 dtr & 6 ch-2 sps)

At the end of Round 3, if you are sewing the Triangles together, fasten off leaving long ends for sewing. If using Join-As-You-Go, do not fasten off.

Designer's Tip: *Even when you're sewing the Triangles together, you can complete Round 4 (without the join-as-you-go) and then sew the loops together, giving your cushion a more lacy and open look.*

JOINING TRIANGLES

Following the layout diagram, either sew the Triangles together, using yarn needle and long ends (or use the Join-As-You-Go method below), to form a Circle.

JOIN-AS-YOU-GO

First Triangle

ROUND 4: Sl st in next 2 dc (to center dc of 5-dcs), ch 1, sc in same st, *ch 3, skip next 2 dc, sc in next sc, ch 3, skip next tr, sc in next (center) tr, ch 3, skip next tr, sc in next ch-2 sp, ch 3, skip next dtr (at point), sc in next ch-2 sp, ch 3, skip next tr, sc in next (center) tr, ch 3, skip next tr, sc in next sc, ch 3, skip next 2 dc**, sc in next dc; rep from * around, ending at ** on final rep; join with sl st to first sc. (21 sc & 21 ch-3 sps) Fasten off.

Second to Fifth Triangles

Rep Round 4 up to first point on Triangle, holding the previous Triangle behind (wrong sides facing), replace the next 8 "ch-3" lps with: ch 1, sl st into corresponding ch-3 lp of previous triangle, ch 1, ending at next point on Triangle. Continue with Round 4 to end. Fasten off.

Sixth Triangle

Rep as before, replacing 15 ch-3 lps with: ch 1, sl st into corresponding ch-3 lp of previous triangle, ch 1, joining two sides of the Triangle, ending at a point. Continue with Round 4 to end. Fasten off.

CUSHION BORDER

ROUND 1: With right side of Circle facing, using smaller hook, join with sl st to any st, crab-st (see Techniques) in each st around (3 crab sts in each ch-3 lp); join with sl st to first sc. Fasten off.

FINISHING CUSHION

Make a fabric cover for the pillow form. Using needle and thread, sew the Cushion to the front of the cover.

Designer's Note:

You could crochet the back cushion cover as well, either by making another identical front piece, or by crocheting a flat circle until it's the same size as the front. Then join the back to the front using crab stitches (see Techniques) all around.

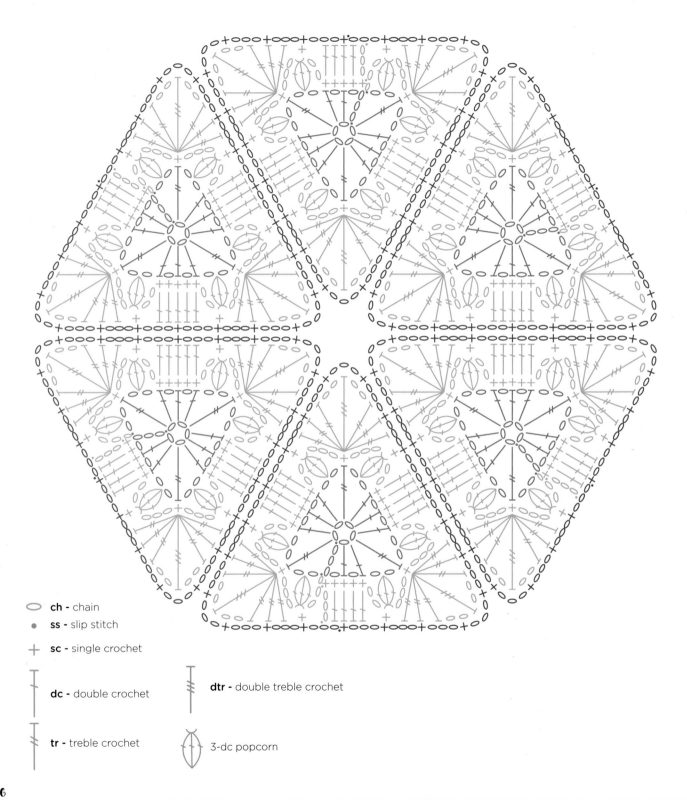

⬭ **ch -** chain	
• **ss -** slip stitch	
+ **sc -** single crochet	
│ **dc -** double crochet	╪ **dtr -** double treble crochet
╪ **tr -** treble crochet	⬭ 3-dc popcorn

Boho Vest

Skill Level
★ ★ ★

This "Boho Vest" is the perfect garment to keep you warm and cozy during chilly days when there's no need to pull out a sweater or cardigan. Add the vintage, hippie look to warm and cozy, and there you have it: good looking and comfortable - a great combination, I think. The pattern for the vest is somewhat challenging, so you might want to try the Boho Cushion first (and practice the Join-As-Go-Method). For the vest we use the same flowery triangles as the Boho Cushion and add half-triangles for the shaping.

Finished Size

To fit average women with hip measurements

40" - 43.5" (102 cm - 111 cm)
Length from shoulder
24 ½" (62 cm)

Width from side to
side (under armholes)
20 ½" (52 cm)

WHAT YOU'LL NEED

❋ **DMC Natura Just Cotton Medium**
Beige (#31) – 12 balls

Hooks:
Size I-9 (5.5 mm)
Size 7 (4.5 mm) – for Panel Edging
Size G-6 (4 mm) – for last round of Panel Edging

Yarn Needle

PATTERN NOTES

❋ Read through the whole pattern first

❋ Do not turn after each round on Triangles

❋ Weave in all ends as you go

Designer's Notes on Sizing:

Measure your hip size and body length.

For a slightly smaller fit, try using a smaller hook. Alternatively, omit Round 4 (the join-as-you-go) of the triangles and half triangles, and sew or crochet the motifs together.

For a slightly larger fit, try adding an extra row (or more) of either single or double crochet stitches across the shoulder (to make longer) and side seams (to make wider) of the panels.

TRIANGLES

ROUNDS 1-3: Using the largest hook, rep Rnds 1-3 of Boho Cushion Triangle.

At the end of Round 3, if you are sewing the Triangles together (for smaller size), fasten off leaving long ends for sewing. If using Join-As-You-Go, do not fasten off.

Join-As-You-Go For Triangles

Designer's Note: *When joining Triangle to Triangle, make sure the right sides are facing.*

The Half-Triangles are not always joined with the right side facing. Sometimes they need to be wrong side facing for the correct fit.

First Triangle (no joining)

ROUND 4: Sl st in next 2 dc (to center dc of 5-dcs), ch 1, sc in same st, *ch 3, skip next 2 dc, sc in next sc, ch 3, skip next tr, sc in next (center) tr, ch 3, skip next tr, sc in next ch-2 sp, ch 3, skip next dtr (at point), sc in next ch-2 sp, ch 3, skip next tr, sc in next (center) tr, ch 3, skip next tr, sc in next sc, ch 3, skip next 2 dc**, sc in next dc; rep from * around, ending at ** on final rep; join with sl st to first sc. (21 sc & 21 ch-3 sps)
Fasten off.

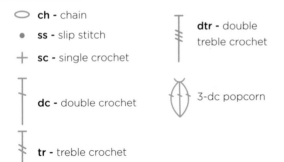

○ **ch** - chain

• **ss** - slip stitch

+ **sc** - single crochet

dc - double crochet

tr - treble crochet

dtr - double treble crochet

3-dc popcorn

Next Triangle(s) (with joining)

When joining, rep Round 4, holding the previous Triangle/Half-Triangle (with open ch-3 lps) behind, replace the "ch-3" lps along the joining side/s with: Ch 1, sl st into corresponding ch-3 lp of previous triangle, ch 1.

Continue with Round 4 to end. Fasten off.

HALF-TRIANGLES

ROW 1: (Right Side) Using the largest hook, ch 23, dc in 4th ch from hook (skipped ch-3 counts as first dc), *dc in next ch; rep from * across. (21 dc)

ROW 2: Ch 5 (counts as first tr & ch-1, now and throughout), skip next dc, tr in next dc, *ch 1, skip next dc, tr in next dc; rep from * twice more (5-tr & 4 sps), dc in each of next 2 dc, hdc in next dc, sc in next dc, sl st in next dc. Leave remaining 7 sts unworked.

ROW 3: Turn, skip sl st, sl st in each of next 5 sts (ending at first tr), ch 1, sc in next ch-1 sp, hdc in next tr, dc in next ch-1 sp, dc in next tr, *tr in next ch-1 sp, tr in next tr; rep from * once more (last tr in 4th ch of ch-5). DO NOT FASTEN OFF.

At the end of Row 3, if you are sewing all the Triangles together, fasten off leaving long ends for sewing. If using Join-As-You-Go, do not fasten off.

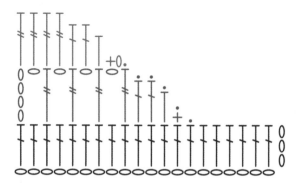

Join-As-You-Go For Half-Triangles

Note: The joining loops are only along the hypotenuse. The other joining side is sewn together.

First Half-Triangle (No Joining)

ROW 4: Ch 3, turn, skip next tr, sc in next tr, ch 3, skip next (tr, dc), sc in next dc, ch 3, skip next (hdc, sc), sc in next tr (from Row 2), ch 3, skip next 2 dc, sc in next hdc, skip next (sc, sl st), sc in next dc (from Row 1), *ch 3, skip next 2 dc, sc in next dc; rep from * once more. Fasten off.

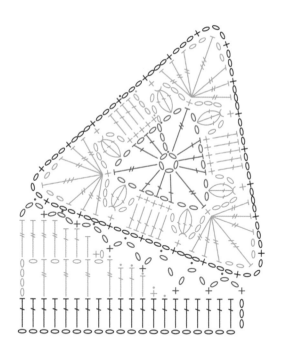

Next Half-Triangle (with joining)

When joining, rep Row 4, holding the previous Triangle (with open ch-3 lps) behind, replace all "ch-3" lps along the joining side/s with: Ch 1, sl st into corresponding ch-3 lp of previous triangle, ch 1, Ending with sc in last dc. Fasten off.

VEST PATTERN

BACK PANEL

Following the layout diagram, make and join 10 Triangles and 4 Half-Triangles to complete the bottom Back panel.

Layout Diagram - Back Panel

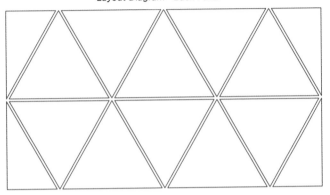

ROW 1: With right side facing, using largest hook, join with sl st to base of first dc (in same) on Half-Triangle, ch 3 (counts as first dc, now and throughout), dc over post of same dc, dc in top of same dc-st, 4 dc in next ch-3 sp, dc in base of next tr (same 4th ch), 3 dc over post of tr, dc in top of same tr, tr in point of next Triangle, ♥ working along next Triangle, 3 dc in next corner ch-sp, *3 dc in next ch-3 lp; rep from * 6 times more, tr in point of next Triangle; rep from ♥ once more, dc in top of next tr, 3 dc over post of same tr, dc in base of same tr, 4 dc in next ch-3 sp, dc in top of next dc, dc over post of same dc, dc in base of same dc (ch-st). (75 sts) Fasten off.

ROW 2: With wrong side facing, skip first 12 dc, join with sl st to next dc, ch 3, dc in each of next 50 dc. (51 dc) Leave remaining 12 dc unworked.

ROWS 3-18: Ch 3, turn, *dc in next dc; rep from * across. (51 dc)

At the end of Row 18, DO NOT FASTEN OFF.

Designer's Hint: To keep the sides of the Back neat, I only make 2 turning chain stitches (instead of the usual chain-3).

First Shoulder

ROW 19: Ch 3, turn, dc in each of next 9 dc. (10 dc) Leave remaining sts unworked.

ROWS 20-21: Ch 3, turn, *dc in next dc; rep from * across. (10 dc)

At the end of Row 21, fasten off.

Second Shoulder

ROW 19: With right side facing, working in Row 18, skip next 27 dc, join with sl st to next dc, ch 3, *dc in next dc; rep from * across. (10 dc)

ROWS 20-21: Ch 3, turn, *dc in next dc; rep from * across. (10 dc)

At the end of Row 21, fasten off and sew in all ends.

Vest - Back Panel

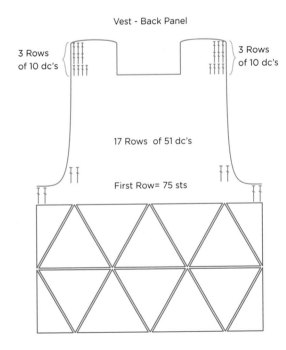

3 Rows of 10 dc's

3 Rows of 10 dc's

17 Rows of 51 dc's

First Row= 75 sts

FRONT PANELS

Following the layout diagrams, join 6 Triangles and 8 Half-Triangles to make each Front. Remember to sew any Half-Triangle sides not joined with loops.

Layout Diagram - Front Panels

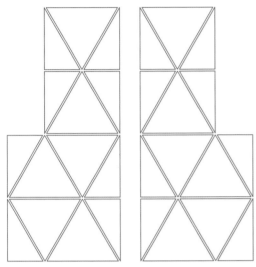

SHOULDER SHAPING

Left Front Shoulder

ROW 1: With right side of Left Front Panel facing, using largest hook, starting at armhole edge, join with sl st to corner ch-3 sp, ch 3 (counts as first dc, now and throughout), 2 dc in same ch-3 sp, *dc in next sc, 2 dc in next ch-3 sp; rep from * 4 times more, sc in next sc, 2 sc in next ch-3 sp, sc in next sc, 3 sc in last corner ch-3 sp. (18 dc, 7 sc) Fasten off.

ROW 2: With right side facing (do not turn), skip first 2 dc, join with sl st to next dc, ch 3, dc in each of next 11 dc. (12 dc) Leave remaining sts unworked. Fasten off.

Left Shoulder Shaping

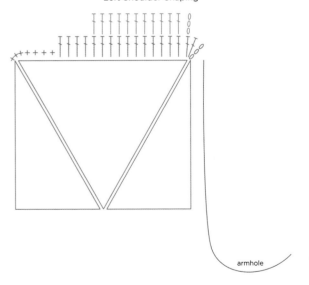

armhole

Right Front Shoulder

ROW 1: With right side of Right Front Panel facing, using largest hook, starting at neck edge, join with sc (see Techniques) in corner ch-3 sp, 2 sc in same sp, sc in next sc, 2 sc in next ch-3 sp, sc in next sc, *2 dc in next ch-3 sp, dc in next sc; rep from * 4 times more, 3 dc in last ch-3 sp. (18 dc, 7 sc) Fasten off.

ROW 2: With right side facing (do not turn), skip first 7 sc, skip next 4 dc, join with sl st to next dc, ch 3, dc in each of next 11 dc. (12 dc) Leave remaining sts unworked. Fasten off.

Right Shoulder Shaping

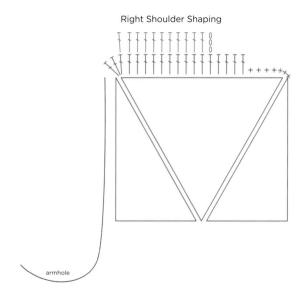

EDGING OF ALL PANELS

Designer's Hint: *Lightly steam-block all three finished panels before starting the edging.*

ROUND 1: With right side facing, using smaller hook, join with sc to any bottom corner at seam, evenly sc around, following the Notes for Edging below; join with sl st to first sc. Remove hook. DO NOT FASTEN OFF.

ROUND 2: Using the smallest hook, sc in each sc around, working 3 sc in center sc of each outer corner; join with sl st to first sc. Fasten off.
Repeat Rounds 1 & 2 on other two panels.

Notes for Edging

1) Work 1 sc in each ch-lp of Half-Triangle.
2) Where two Half-Triangles are joined, work sc3tog - using the last st of current Half-Triangle, the st in the join, and the first st of next Half-Triangle
3) On outer corners, work 3 sc in same st
4) At the inner corners of armholes, on Fronts, working in sides of rows of Half-Triangle, sc across to last tr, 3 sc over post of last tr, hdc in top last tr, dc3tog – using loops from next 3 adjacent triangles, hdc in next Half-Triangle, sc across as before.

Inner Corners of Armholes

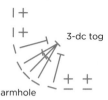

5) For the inner corners of the Back, sc to last 2 sts (or last row), hdc in next st (or row), dc3tog – using next st (or same row), corner and side of row (or next st), sc across as before.
6) In the unused join-as-you-go sides on Triangles, work an sc in each sc, and 2 sc in each ch-3 sp.
7) On the Back Panel, working in the sides of rows, work 2 sc over post of each dc.

Designer's Note: *For the Edging, the stitch count is not important. What matters is that the panels lie flat.*

ASSEMBLY OF VEST

Position and pin the seams of the three panels. Join each shoulder seam, then join the side seams, using any method you choose. Block the completed Vest before wearing.

Designer's Hint: *I used the flat zipper join (see Techniques) on the shoulder seams, making the seams lay beautifully flat. The side seams I sewed up using needle and yarn.*

Childhood Poncho "Sem"

Skill Level

*

My very first piece of crochet was a poncho in pink, green and off-white, which I made when I was nine years old. Both my mom and I vividly remember me crocheting it, as well as the poncho itself - even though it's been missing for many, many years (and we have no idea where it is). Ever since I started crocheting again in 2010 my thoughts have gone back to this first project, and for years I've wanted to re-create it.
A bit nostalgic, I know, but crocheting my childhood poncho again, knowing sweet Sem would model it for me, made this new poncho extra special. The cherry on the cake was, after the photo shoot, Sem asking me to teach her how to crochet!

Finished Size

To fit average 8-10
year old child

Length down mid-front
21" (53 cm)

Width across at widest
point 28 ½" (72 cm)

WHAT YOU'LL NEED

✱ DMC Natura Just Cotton
Pink (N62 Cerise) – 4 balls
Off-White (N35 Nacar) – 2 balls
Green (N54 Green Smoke) – 1 ball

Hook: Size E-4 (3.5 mm)

Yarn Needle

PATTERN NOTES

✱ Do not turn after each round

✱ Fasten off after each color change

✱ Weave in all ends as you go

Designer's Notes On Sizing:

The basis of the pattern is the Granny Square Neckline, so it is fairly easy to adjust the sizing. You can make a smaller or bigger Poncho by either omitting or adding rounds of 3-dc groups to the Granny Square, or even increasing or decreasing the number of Granny Squares needed.

For the colorful, smaller sized poncho, I made ten Granny Squares of 3-rounds each. I then added only 18 rounds for the poncho, using a different color for each round to create stripes.

The finished size for this smaller Poncho fits an average 4-6 year old.

Length down mid-front - 13" (32 cm); and width across at widest point – 19" (48 cm)

NECKLINE GRANNY SQUARES – Make 10

ROUND 1: (Right Side) Using Off-White, ch 4, join with sl st to first ch to form a ring (or start with a Magic Ring - see Techniques); ch 5 (counts as first dc & ch-2, now and throughout), *3 dc in ring, ch 2; rep from * twice more, 2 dc in ring; join with sl st to first dc (3rd ch of beg ch-5). (4 groups of 3-dc each & 4 corner ch-2 sps) Fasten off Off-White.

ROUND 2: With right side facing, join Green with sl st to any corner ch-2 sp, ch 5, 3 dc in same sp, *(3 dc, ch 2, 3 dc) in next ch-2 sp; rep from * around, ending with 2 dc in same first corner ch-2 sp; join with sl st to first dc. (8 groups of 3-dc each & 4 corner ch-2 sps) Fasten off Green.

Designer's Tip: *When starting a new round with a new color, I do not use the "chain 3" as my first dc. Instead, I crochet a "standing double crochet" (see Techniques). This is just my personal preference.*

ROUND 3: With right side facing, join Pink with sl st to any corner ch-2 sp, ch 5, 3 dc in same sp, 3 dc in sp between next two 3-dc groups, *(3 dc, ch 2, 3 dc) in next ch-2 sp, 3 dc in sp between next two 3-dc groups; rep from * around, ending with 2 dc in same first corner ch-2 sp; join with sl st to first dc. (12 groups of 3-dc each & 4 corner ch-2 sps) Fasten off Pink.

ROUND 4: With right side facing, join Off-White with sl st to any ch-2 corner, ch 5, 3 dc in same sp, [3 dc in next sp between groups] twice, *(3 dc, ch 2, 3 dc) in next ch-2 sp, [3 dc in next sp between groups] twice; rep from * around, ending with 2 dc in same first corner ch-2 sp; join with sl st to first dc. (16 groups of 3-dc each & 4 corner ch-2 sps) Fasten off Off-White.

Finishing the Neckline

Repeat Rounds 1-4 for the remaining 9 squares.

Following the layout diagram, sew or crochet the 10 squares together.

Designer's Hint: *If you want, you can use the "join-as-you-go" method (see Techniques) on Round 4.*

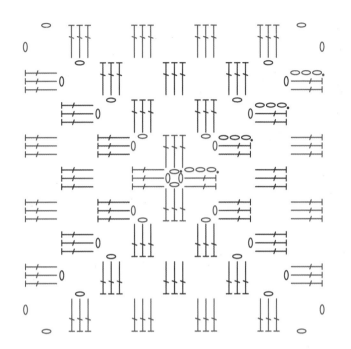

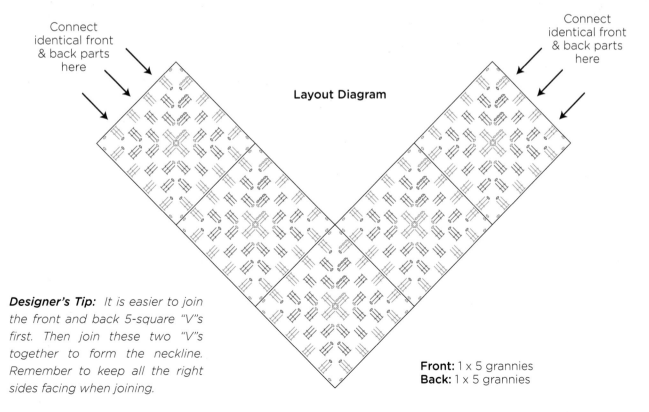

Layout Diagram

Connect identical front & back parts here

Connect identical front & back parts here

Designer's Tip: *It is easier to join the front and back 5-square "V"s first. Then join these two "V"s together to form the neckline. Remember to keep all the right sides facing when joining.*

Front: 1 x 5 grannies
Back: 1 x 5 grannies

PONCHO

ROUND 1: With right side of completed Neckline facing, join Pink with sl st to either of the outer corner ch-2 sps (at the point of the "V"), ch 5, 3 dc in same sp, *[3 dc in next sp between groups] 3 times, 3 dc in next ch-2 sp (of current square), 3 dc in next ch-2 sp (of next square); rep from * 4 times more, [3 dc in next sp between groups] 3 times**, (3 dc, ch 2, 3 dc) in next corner ch-2 sp; rep from * to ** once, 2 dc in same first corner ch-2 sp; join with sl st to first dc (3rd ch of beg ch-5). (60 dc-groups – 30 each side & 2 corner ch-2 sps)

ROUND 2: Continuing with Pink, sl st in next ch (of corner ch-2), ch 5, 3 dc in same ch-2 sp, [3 dc in next sp between groups] around, working (3 dc, ch 2, 3 dc) in next corner ch-2 sp, ending with 2 dc in same first corner sp; join with sl st to first dc. (62 dc-groups – 31 each side & 2 corner ch-2 sps)

ROUND 3: Rep Rnd 2. (64 dc-groups – 32 each side & 2 corner ch-2 sps) Fasten off Pink.

ROUND 4: With right side facing, join Off-White to corner ch-2 sp, ch 5, 3 dc in same ch-2 sp, [3 dc in next sp between groups] around, working (3 dc, ch 2, 3 dc) in next corner ch-2 sp, ending with 2 dc in same first corner sp; join with sl st to first dc. (66 dc-groups – 33 each side & 2 corner ch-2 sps) Fasten off Off-White.

ROUND 5: With right side facing, join Green to corner ch-2 sp, ch 5, 3 dc in same ch-2 sp, [3 dc in next sp between groups] around, working (3 dc, ch 2, 3 dc) in next corner ch-2 sp, ending with 2 dc in same first corner sp; join with sl st to first dc. (68 dc-groups – 34 each side & 2 corner ch-2 sps) Fasten off Green.

ROUND 6: With right side facing, join Off-White to corner ch-2 sp, ch 5, 3 dc in same ch-2 sp, [3 dc in next sp between groups] around, working (3 dc, ch 2, 3 dc) in next corner ch-2 sp, ending with 2 dc in same first corner sp; join with sl st to first dc. (70 dc-groups – 35 each side & 2 corner ch-2 sps) Fasten off Off-White.

ROUND 7: With right side facing, join Pink to corner ch-2 sp, ch 5, 3 dc in same ch-2 sp, [3 dc in next sp between groups] around, working (3 dc, ch 2, 3 dc) in next corner ch-2 sp, ending with 2 dc in same first corner sp; join with sl st to first dc. (72 dc-groups – 36 each side & 2 corner ch-2 sps)

ROUNDS 8-10: Rep Rnd 2. At the end of Rnd 10 (4 rounds of Pink), there are 78 dc-groups – 39 each side & 2 corner ch-2 sps. Fasten off Pink.

ROUNDS 11-14: Rep Rnds 4-7.

ROUNDS 15-18: Rep Rnd 2. At the end of Rnd 18 (5 rounds of Pink), there are 94 dc-groups – 47 each side & 2 corner ch-2 sps. Fasten off Pink.

ROUNDS 19-22: Rep Rnds 4-7.

ROUNDS 23-27: Rep Rnd 2.

At the end of Rnd 27 (6 rounds of Pink), there are 112 dc-groups – 56 each side & 2 corner ch-2 sps. Fasten off Pink.

ROUNDS 28-31: Rep Rnds 4-7.

ROUNDS 32-34: Rep Rnd 2.

At the end of Rnd 34 (4 rounds of Pink), there are 124 dc-groups – 62 each side & 2 corner ch-2 sps. Fasten off Pink.

PONCHO BORDER

ROUND 1: With right side facing, using Off-White, join with sc (see Techniques) to corner ch-2 sp, ch 1, sc in same sp, ch 1, [skip next dc, sc in next (center) dc, ch 1, skip next dc, sc in sp between groups, ch 1] around, working ([sc, ch 1] twice) in next corner ch-2 sp; join with sl st to first sc. Fasten off Off-White.

ROUND 2: With right side facing, using Green, join with sc to any ch-1 sp, ch 1, [sc in next ch-1 sp, ch 1] around, working ([sc, ch 1] twice) in each corner; join with sl st to first sc. Fasten off Green.

NECK EDGING

ROUND 1: With right side facing, working inside the Neckline, join Off-White with sc to center back ch-2 sp, ch 1, sc in next ch-2 sp (of next square), ch 1, [skip next dc, sc in next (center) dc, ch 1, skip next dc, sc in sp between groups, ch 1] around, working (sc, ch 1) in each ch-2 sp (of adjoining squares); join with sl st to first sc. Fasten off Off-White.

ROUND 2: With right side facing, using Green, join with sc to any ch-1 sp, ch 1, [sc in next ch-1 sp, ch 1] around; join with sl st to first sc. Fasten off Green.

Cobblestone Blanket

Skill Level
*

This is another easy pattern with great looks. The stitches give the blanket a nice, textured feel. Adapting the size to your personal preference is not complicated at all, so for a stroller blanket, a baby blanket, or anything bigger, here's your go-to pattern.

Finished Size

Blanket measures about
31 ½" (80 cm) wide by
47 ¼" (120 cm) long

WHAT YOU'LL NEED

✳ **DMC Natura Just Cotton Medium**
Light Grey (#12) - 20 balls
Yellow (#09) - 1 ball (for the Border)

Hooks:
Size K-10½ (7 mm) for Blanket
Size I-9 (5.5 mm) for Border

Yarn Needle

PATTERN NOTES

✳ The stitch pattern has a multiple of "3"

✳ The three stitches in the group (sc, hdc & dc) are all worked together in one stitch

✳ From Row 2 onwards, each group of stitches is worked only in the sc-st of the previous row; the hdc- and dc-sts of the previous row are skipped

✳ Weave in all ends as you go

Designer's Note: *You can adapt the width of the blanket to any size. Just make sure the number of chain stitches you start with is divisible by 3.*

SPECIAL STITCHES

Puff Stitch (puff): In same st or sp indicated, [yo hook, insert hook, pull up a loop (to height of hdc)] 3 times (7 loops on hook), yo and draw through all 7 loops on the hook, ch 1 (to lock) (puff stitch made).

BLANKET

ROW 1: (Right Side) Using Grey and larger hook, ch 111, (hdc, dc) in 3rd ch from hook, skip next 2 chs, *(sc, hdc, dc) in next ch, skip next 2 ch; rep from * across to last ch, sc in last ch. (35 groups of 3-sts, 1 group of 2-sts & 1 sc)

ROW 2: Ch 2, turn, (hdc, dc) in first sc, skip next 2 sts, *(sc, hdc, dc) in next sc, skip next 2 sts; rep from * across, ending with sc in ch-2 sp. (35 groups of 3-sts, 1 group of 2-sts & 1 sc)

ROWS 3 TO 104 (or to desired length): Rep Row 2, ending on an even-numbered row. At the end of the last row, fasten off Grey.

BORDER

ROUND 1: With right side facing, using Yellow and smaller hook, join with sc (see Techniques) to first sc (last sc worked on final row), *ch 3, puff (see Special Stitches) in 3rd ch from hook, skip next 2 sts, sc in next sc; rep from * across, working last sc in ch-2 sp, **working in sides of rows, [ch 3, puff in 3rd ch from hook, skip next row, sc in next ch-2 sp] across to next corner**, working last sc in first skipped ch-2 sp on foundation ch, working in sps on starting ch, [ch 3, puff in 3rd ch from hook, sc in next sp] across, working the last sc in the first ch-2 turning ch; rep from ** to ** once, omitting last sc on final rep; join with sl st to first ch. Fasten off Yellow.

⬭ **ch -** chain

✛ **sc -** single crochet

| **hdc -** half double crochet

† **dc -** double crochet

⬭ puff stitch

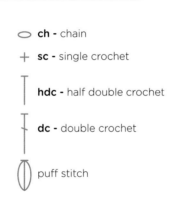
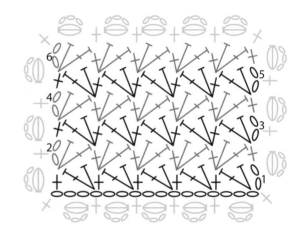

Corner-to-Corner Cushion "Anneke"

Skill Level

*

I've used the so-called "corner-to-corner" technique (C2C) several times already, and I'm a big fan! It's a great way to create pixelated work, allowing you to crochet images into your work. Counted cross stitch designs are very suitable to use in combination with C2C-crochet, as are geometrical designs, which is what I've opted for in this pattern. As you're crocheting your squares, you'll see you have even more lay-out options than the one given here!

Finished Size

To fit a 20" (50 cm)
square pillow form

Each motif square
measures 4 ¾" by 4 ¾"
(12 cm by 12 cm)

WHAT YOU'LL NEED

✻ DMC Natura Just Cotton Medium

Color A (#126) - 3 balls
Color B (#134) - 3 balls
Color C (#198) - 3 balls

Designer's Note: *For The Pastel version, I used: Color A (#07), Color B (#03) and Color C (#04), with a little of Color #444 for the first round of the border, instead of Color A.*

Hooks:
Size I-9 (5.5 mm) for Motif Squares
Size 7 (4.5 mm) for Border

Yarn Needle

Pillow Form - 20" square

Fabric - to cover pillow form

Needle and matching thread

PATTERN NOTES

✻ Fasten off after each color change

✻ Weave in all ends as you go

Designer's Note: *Corner-to-corner (C2C) is a technique worked up using crocheted 'blocks' on the diagonal - from one corner, increasing each row until the desired size, then decreasing each row to the opposite corner.*

48

MOTIF SQUARE – Make 16

ROW 1: (Right Side) Using Color A and larger hook, ch 6, dc in 4th ch from hook, dc in each of next 2 ch (first block made). (1 block)

Designers Hint: *The starting yarn tail is the first corner point.*

Increase Rows

ROW 2: Ch 6, turn, dc in 4th ch from hook, dc in each of next 2 ch (second block made), skip next 3 dc, sl st in next ch-3 sp, ch 3, 3 dc in same ch-3 sp (third block made). (2 blocks)

ROW 3: Ch 6, turn, dc in 4th ch from hook, dc in each of next 2 ch, *skip next 3 dc, sl st in next ch-3 sp, ch 3, 3 dc in same ch-3 sp (of 3rd block made in Row 2); rep from * into 2nd block made in Row 2. (3 blocks)

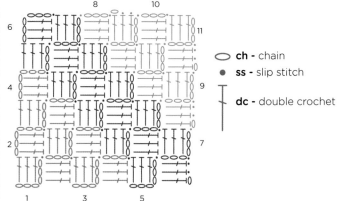

ch - chain
ss - slip stitch
dc - double crochet

ROW 4: Ch 6, turn, dc in 4th ch from hook, dc in each of next 2 ch, *skip next 3 dc, sl st in next ch-3 sp, ch 3, 3 dc in same ch-3 sp; rep from * across. (4 blocks) Fasten off Color A.

ROW 5: With right side facing, using Color B, ·join with sl st to last dc on the last block worked, ch 6, turn, dc in 4th ch from hook, dc in each of next 2 ch, *skip next 3 dc, sl st in next ch-3 sp, ch 3, 3 dc in same ch-3 sp; rep from * across. (5 blocks)

ROW 6: Rep Row 4. DO NOT FASTEN OFF.

At the end of Row 6, there are 6 blocks along each edge.

Designers Hint: *Row numbers are counted by counting the 'blocks' along each edge.*

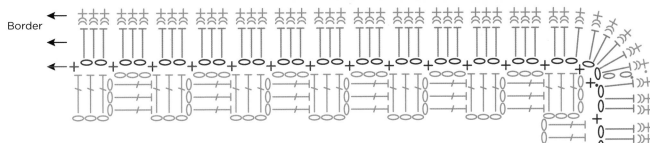

Border

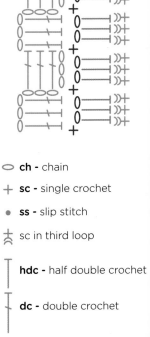

Decrease Rows

ROW 7: Ch 1, turn, sl st in each of next 2 dc, *sl st in next ch-3 sp, ch 3, 3 dc in same ch-3 sp, skip next 3 dc; rep from * across, ending with sl st in last ch-3 sp. (5 blocks) Fasten off Color B.

ROW 8: With wrong side facing, using Color C, skip last 3 dc worked on Row 7, join with *sl st to next ch-3 sp, ch 3, to next ch-3 sp, ch 3, 3 dc in same ch-3 sp, skip next 3 dc; rep from * across, ending with sl st in last ch-3 sp. (4 blocks)

ROWS 9-10: Ch 1, turn, sl st in each of next 2 dc, *sl st in next ch-3 sp, ch 3, 3 dc in same ch-3 sp, skip next 3 dc; rep from * across, ending with sl st in last ch-3 sp. At the end of Row 10, there are 2 blocks.

ROW 11: Ch 1, turn, sl st in each of next 2 dc, sl st in next ch-3 sp, ch 3, 3 dc in same ch-3 sp, skip next 3 dc, sl st in last ch-3 sp. (1 block) Fasten off Color C.

Designer's Tip: *In this project I left (very) long yarn ends when fastening off my motif squares, and then used them to sew the squares together.*

ASSEMBLY OF SQUARES
use photo as guide

After all 16 squares are finished, lay them out in a 4 x 4 grid, creating a geometric design, either using the one in the photo, or your own design. Using the long ends and yarn needle, sew all the squares together.

BORDER

ROUND 1: Holding assembled grid, using Color B and smaller hook, join with sc (see Techniques) to any corner st, ch 2, sc in same corner, ch 2, *skip dc-st/s, sc in sp between blocks, ch 2; rep from * around, working (sc, ch 2, sc) in each corner; join with sl st to first sc. Fasten off Color B.

ROUND 2: With right side facing, join Color A with sl st to any corner ch-2 sp, ch 2, 5 hdc in same sp, *3 hdc in next ch-2 sp; rep from * around, working 5 hdc in each corner ch-2 sp; join with sl st to first hdc. Fasten off Color A.

ROUND 3: With right side facing, using Color C, join with sc to third loop (see Techniques) of any hdc in Rnd 2, working in third loops only, sc in each hdc around; join with sl st to first sc. Fasten off Color C.

ASSEMBLY OF CUSHION

Using the fabric, make a pillow case to fit over the pillow form. Position the crocheted piece on the front of the fabric cover and using needle and thread, sew in place.

Designer's Note: *I found a lovely light pink gingham fabric in my stash and machine sewed it together in an envelope style cover onto which I hand stitched my crochet cushion front.*

○ **ch** - chain

+ **sc** - single crochet

• **ss** - slip stitch

⋏ sc in third loop

| **hdc** - half double crochet

‡ **dc** - double crochet

Dolly Dotty Cushion

Playing with color is one of my very favorite crafty things to do, and it's probably the main reason I like crochet as much as I do. No boundaries, rules, or restrictions - simply trying out all kinds of different colors, until the "Oooh, I like that!" moment pops up... I love it! In the "Dolly Dotty" Cushion, I not only played with colors, but with shapes as well - turning circles into squares. Have fun playing!

Finished Size

Front of cushion – About 15" (40 cm) square

Each Motif measures 3" (8 cm) square

WHAT YOU'LL NEED

✱ **DMC Natura Just Cotton**
Main Color (MC): Off-White (N35 Nacar) – 2 balls
Color A & Color B – small amounts of many colors

Designer's Note: For Colors A & B, use any combination of colors which tickles your fancy. I used almost all the colors I worked with for my Granny Square Cardigan "Marie", plus some more extra colors I had lying around.

Hooks:
Size E-4 (3.5 mm) for Motifs
Size C-2 (2.75 mm) for Border

Yarn Needle

Pillow Form – 16" square

Fabric to cover pillow form

Needle and matching thread

PATTERN NOTES

✱ Do not turn after each round

✱ Fasten off after each color change

✱ Weave in all ends as you go

Designer's Tip: On round 4, make sure to work a dc in all stitches from round 3, including the first tr after each corner. It's hiding a bit under the corner stitches, but needs its own dc to get four nice, straigt sides on your squares.

MOTIF – Make 25

ROUND 1: (Right Side) Using Color A and larger hook, ch 6; join with sl st to first ch to form ring (or use Magic Ring – see Techniques); ch 3 (counts as first dc, now and throughout), 23 dc in ring; join with sl st to first dc (3rd ch of beg ch-3). (24 dc) Fasten off Color A.

ROUND 2: With right side facing, using Color B, join with sc (see Techniques) to any dc, ch 2, skip next dc, *sc in next dc, ch 2, skip next dc; rep from * around; join with sl st to first sc. (12 sc & 12 ch-2 sps)

ROUND 3: Sl st in next ch-2 sp, ch 3, (4 tr, dc) in same ch-2 sp (first corner made), *skip next sc, 2 dc in next ch-2 sp, dc in next sc, 2 dc in next ch-2 sp, skip next sc**, (dc, 4 tr, dc) in next ch-2 sp; rep from * around, ending at ** on final repeat; join with sl st to first dc. (16 tr & 28 dc - 11 sts on each side) Fasten off Color B.

ROUND 4: With right side facing, join MC with sl st to any st, ch 3, dc in every st around, working (2 dc, ch 2, 2 dc) in sp between center 2 tr of 4-tr group; join with sl st to first dc. (60 dc – 15 on each side - & 4 corner ch-2 sps) Fasten off MC.

⬭	**ch** - chain
•	**ss** - slip stitch
+	**sc** - single crochet
⊤	**dc** - double crochet
⫠	**tr** - treble crochet

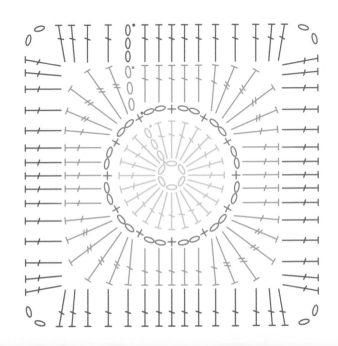

ASSEMBLY OF MOTIFS

Position the 25 Motifs in a 5 by 5 grid to determine your color design. First join motifs into strips of 5 motifs each. Then join the 5 strips together.

Designer's Note: The different options for joining are: 1. Sewing the motifs together (either using both loops or, for a more decorative line, using the back loops only); or 2. Crocheting them together (using either sl st or sc-sts). My favorite method is the crocheted zipper stitch (see Techniques), which is quick to do and keeps everything flat.

BORDER

ROUND 1: With right side of cushion facing, using MC and smaller hook, surface stitch (see Techniques) in each dc and ch around. Fasten off.

Designer's Note: I felt this cushion did not need a frilly, colorful border. So, I added surface stitches (see Techniques) all around the piece in the last round, right beneath the little "v" showing on top of each dc (but not around the post). At the intersection of 2 motifs, where I had a flat zipper join, I first slip stitched a stitch into the first corner of the first motif, then inserted my hook right into the heart of the zipper join that sat between the two corners of adjoining motifs, and made the next stitch there, with the next stitch in the corner of the following motif.

FINISHING CUSHION

Make a fabric cover for the pillow form. Using needle and thread, sew the Cushion to the front of the cover.

Designer's Note: If you wanted to, you could crochet a cushion back piece, making it the same size as the Front, and then sew join the Front and Back together. Or you can just sew the crocheted Front to a store-bought cushion cover.

Flowers in a Field Shawl, Cushion & Flower Garland

Skill Level
**

Flowers in a field is exactly what this pattern reminds me of. I crocheted the shawl using the lovely, soft DMC Woolly (100% Merino wool), and it is such a joy to wear. I couldn't help myself, and crocheted some more of these motifs using DMC Natura Just Cotton Medium as well, using all kinds of pretty and bright colors. I turned these motifs into a happy, flowery cushion cover. With the left-over colorful flowers, I created a garland, adding some leaves. (You'll find that pattern here too). These floral motifs are actually granny squares, but when you use one color for the last three rounds, the seams/sides of the granny squares seem to disappear... Quite the surprise!

Finished Size

Shawl – About 16 ½" (42 cm) wide by 60 ½" (154 cm) long

Cushion Cover – About 16 ½" (42 cm) square

Flower Garland - About 48" (180 cm) long

Each Motif measures 5 ½" (14 cm) square

WHAT YOU'LL NEED

For Shawl:

✳ **DMC Woolly**
Main Color – MC (#065) – 3 balls
Color A (#01) – 1 ball
Color B (#101) – 2 balls

Hook: Size I-9 (5.5 mm)

Yarn Needle

For Cushion Cover & Flower Garland:

✳ **DMC Natura Just Cotton Medium**
Main Color (MC) – Any color/s of your choice.
Color A and Color B: Mix and match your own choice of colors.

Designer's Note: *For the Cushion Cover and Flower Garland, I used the following colors: #01, #03, #05, #09, #44, #77, #99, #109, #126, #134, #198, #444, #700*
For the Garland, I added #12 and #41.
For the leaves I used #198.

Hook: Size H-8 (5 mm)

Yarn Needle

Needle and matching thread (for Flower Garland)

PATTERN NOTES

✳ Do not turn after each round

✳ Fasten off after each color change

✳ Weave in all ends as you go

SPECIAL STITCHES

Bobble Stitch (bob): Yarn over hook twice, insert hook in st or sp indicated and pull up a loop, [yarn over and draw through 2 loops on hook] twice (2 loops remain on hook). *Yarn over twice and insert hook in same stich and pull up a loop, [yarn over draw through 2 loops on hook] twice; rep from * once more; yarn over, draw through all remaining loops on hook (bobble made).

FLORAL MOTIF

Flower

ROUND 1: (Right Side) Using Color A, ch 4, join with sl st to first ch to form ring (or use Magic Ring (see Techniques); ch 4 (counts as first dc & ch-1, now and throughout), *dc in ring, ch 1; rep from * 6 times more; join with sl st to first dc (3rd ch of beg ch-4). (8 dc & 8 ch-1 sps) Fasten off Color A.

ROUND 2: With right side facing, join Color B with sl st to any ch-1 sp, ch 3, (bob (see Special Stitches), ch 3, sl st) in same sp, *(sl st, ch 3, bob, ch 3, sl st) in next ch-1 sp; rep from * around; join with sl st to first sl st. (8 petals) Fasten off Color B.

For Flower Garland, continue with Flower Garland Assembly.

For Shawl and Cushion Cover, continue with Motif Edging

Motif Edging

ROUND 3: With right side facing, using MC, join with sc (see Techniques) to any bobble, *ch 3, dc (loosely, so it remains the same height as the sc) in sl st between petals, ch 3**, sc in next bobble; rep from * around, ending at ** on final repeat; join with sl st to first sc. (8 sc, 8 dc & 16 ch-3 sps)

ROUND 4: Sl st in each of next 2 ch (of ch-3 sp), ch 1, sc in same ch-3 sp, ch 4, *sc in next ch-3 sp, ch 4; rep from * around; join with sl st to first sc. (16 sc & 16 ch-4 lps) DO NOT FASTEN OFF.

For First Motif Only

ROUND 5 (Joining Round): Sl st in each of next 2 ch (of ch-4 lp), ch 1, sc in same ch-4 lp, ch 4, [sc in next ch-4 lp, ch 4] twice, *(dc, ch 3, dc) in next ch-4 lp (corner made), ch4**, [sc in next ch-4 lp, ch 4] 3 times, rep from * around, ending at ** on final repeat; join with sl st to first sc. (12 sc, 8 dc, 16 ch-4 lps & 4 ch-3 sps) Fasten off MC.

For Join-As-You-Go Motifs

Rep Round 5, but on the side/s that are to be joined, starting at the corner, holding the previous Motif behind (right sides facing), work as follows: dc in next ch-4 lp, ch 1, working in previous Motif, sl st in corresponding ch-3 sp, ch 1, working in current Motif, dc in same ch-4 lp, *ch 2, working in previous Motif, sl st in corresponding ch-4 lp, ch 2, sc in next ch-4 lp; rep from * twice more, ch 2, working in previous Motif, sl st in corresponding ch-4 lp, ch 2, dc in next ch-4 lp, ch 1, working in previous Motif, sl st in corresponding ch-3 sp, ch 1, working in current Motif, dc in same ch-4 lp; continue with the Round as established.

Designer's Tip: *When you attach 3 or 4 Motifs together, at the corner(s) where they all join, sl st into the sl st previously made (the join of the first two Motifs). You can identify this as a little "v" stitch, facing you horizontally.*

FLOWERS IN A FIELD SHAWL

For the Shawl, make 33 complete Floral Motifs, joining them together in a strip, 3 motifs wide by 11 motifs long.

FLOWERS IN A FIELD CUSHION COVER

For the Cushion Cover, make 9 complete Floral Motifs, using any combination of colors for each Motif, joining them together in a 3- by 3-motif square.

FLOWER GARLAND

For the Flower Garland, make 20 Flowers (Floral Motif - Rounds 1 & 2 only) using any combination of colors for each Flower. Make 10 Big Leaves and 6 Small Leaves.

Big Leaf – Make 10

Using any leaf color, ch 10, sl st in 2nd ch from hook, *sc in next ch, hdc in next ch, dc in next ch, tr in next ch, dc in next ch, hdc in next ch, sc in next ch, sl st in last ch*, ch 1, working in unused lps on other side of starting ch, sl st in next ch; rep from * to * once. Fasten off.

Small Leaf – Make 6

Using any leaf color, ch 8, sl st in 2nd ch from hook, *sc in next ch, hdc in next ch, dc in next ch, hdc in next ch, sc in next ch, sl st in last ch*, ch 1, working in unused lps on other side of starting ch, sl st in next ch; rep from * to * once. Fasten off and weave in ends.

Flower Garland Assembly

Using Off-White (#03), ch 40, working in a Flower, *sl st in the back of any petal, ch 3, sl st in the back of the next petal (same Flower), ch 12, working in the next Flower; rep from * until all Flowers are connect, ch 40. Fasten off.

Hand sew the leaves with needle and thread to the back of some of the flowers.

Designer's Tip: *If you want, you can embellish some (or all) of your leaves by using a contrasting color to add surface stitches - either around the edge of the leaf, or down the 'spine' of the leaf, or both.*

ch - chain
- **ss -** slip stitch
+ **sc -** single crochet

dc - double crochet

bob - 3-tr bobble

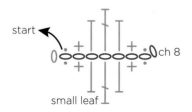

start

ch 8

small leaf

start

ch 10

big leaf

ch - chain
- **ss -** slip stitch
+ **sc -** single crochet

hdc - half double crochet

dc - double crochet

tr - treble crochet

Geometric Triangle Blanket

Skill Level
★ ★

I love geometric patterns, especially in crochet. There was no doubt in my mind that I would use black and white in this blanket, nor that I would add a whimsical - and very pink - touch to it. Of course, you can use any color combination you like, thus easily making this design your very own. I'm so pleased to see the design works really well using lots of different colors too!

Finished Size

Blanket measures about
33 ½" (85 cm) wide by
37 ½" (95 cm) long

WHAT YOU'LL NEED

✻ **DMC Natura Just Cotton Medium**

For the Black & White Blanket:
Black (#02) - 7 balls
White (#01) - 5 balls
Pink (#444) - 1 ball

For the Colorful Blanket:
Off-White (#03) - 6 balls
Various colors (#04, #05, #07, #09, #10, #41, #44, #77, #99, #109, #126, #134, #177, #198, #444, #700) - 1 ball each

Hooks:
Size H-8 (5 mm) for blanket
Size G-6 (4 mm) for border

Yarn Needle

PATTERN NOTES

✻ The pattern is written for the Black & White blanket. (For the colorful blanket, use Off-White for every odd-numbered row and use a different color for each even-numbered row)

✻ Fasten off after each color change

✻ Weave in all ends as you go

Designer's Note: *It's easy to adjust the size of this blanket. The pattern has a chain multiple of 6 + 2. So start with any length of chain you like. Just make sure it is divisible by 6. Then add 2 extra chains (one for the turning chain and one for the last stitch). I started with a chain of 122, which gave my blanket 20 black/white little boxes.*

BLANKET

Designer's Note: *The pattern automatically gives your blanket loops on both sides, as well as along the bottom; the loops on top are worked in the last row.*

ROW 1: With Black and larger hook, ch 122, sc in 2nd ch from hook, *ch 6, working in ch-6, sc in 2nd ch from hook, hdc in next ch, dc in next ch, tr in next ch, dtr in last ch; working in starting ch, skip next 5 ch-sts, sc in next ch; rep from * across to end, ch 5, turn, skip next 4 sts (of last triangle worked), sc in last sc, changing color to White (see Techniques). (20 triangles)

ROW 2: ROW 2: With White, *working in unused ch-lps of ch-6, sc in first ch, hdc in next ch, dc in next ch, tr in next ch, dtr in last ch**, skip next 5 sts (sc, dtr, tr, dc, hdc - on next triangle), sc in last sc; rep from * across, ending at ** on final repeat, 1 dtr in last st, changing color to Black in last st. (20 B&W blocks)

ROW 3: With Black, turn, sc in last dtr made in row 2, *ch 6, sc in 2nd ch from hook, hdc in next ch, dc in next ch, tr in next ch, dtr in last ch; working in previous row, skip next 5 sts, sc in next sc (at tip of triangle); rep from * across to end, ch 5, skip next 4 sts (of last triangle worked), sc in last sc, changing color to White. (20 triangles)

ROWS 4-46 (Or To Desired Length): Rep Rows 2-3, ending on Row 2.

ROW 47 (Or Last Row): With Black, ch 1, turn, sc in first dtr, ch 5, skip next 4 sts, sc in next sc (at tip of triangle), *ch 5, skip next 5 sts, sc in next sc; rep from * across. DO NOT FASTEN OFF.

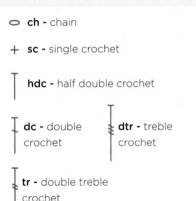

⬭ **ch -** chain

\+ **sc -** single crochet

hdc - half double crochet

dc - double crochet

dtr - treble crochet

tr - double treble crochet

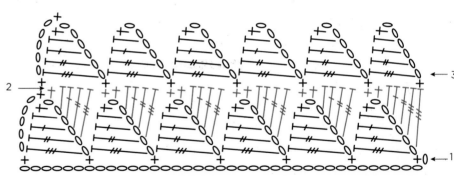

Designer's Note: *At the beginning, this pattern may feel a bit fiddly but once you have the hang of crocheting these nifty triangle stitches, it becomes a lovely "I'm-in-a-crochet-flow" kind of pattern.*

While crocheting your blanket, you might see it turn and twist a bit askew, giving the blanket a somewhat diamond-like shape (instead of square). Sewing your ends in rather tightly and blocking this beauty (definitely a must) will mostly take care of that, but the sides on this blanket will never be perfectly straight.

BORDER

ROUND 1: (Right Side) With Black, 2 sc in same st (as last sc worked – first corner made), sc evenly around, working 5 sc in each lp (either ch 5 or dtr), sc between lps (around all sides of blanket) and 3 sc in each corner; join with sl st to first sc. Fasten off Black.

ROUND 2: With right side facing, join Pink with sl st to center sc of any 3-sc corner, ch 3 (counts as first dc), 2 dc in same sc, ♥ hdc in next sc, *sc in next sc, hdc in next sc, dc in next sc, hdc in next sc, sc in next sc**, sl st in next sc; rep from * across side, ending at ** on final repeat, hdc in next sc ♥♥, 3 dc in next sc (corner made); rep from ♥ around, ending at ♥♥ on final repeat; join with sl st to first dc (3rd ch of beg ch-3). Fasten off Pink.

Designer's Tip: *Remember to gently steam-block your blanket to straighten the sides.*

Giant Granny Square Blanket "Anne"

Skill Level
*

To me this project can be characterized as "Easy pattern", "A joy to crochet", and "Great and quick result". Crocheting this cheerful, warm blanket - that as you can see, would work extremely well as a rug too - was a very pleasurable ride. Adding the tassels to the mix, with all the wonderful colors, gives the "Giant Granny" a somewhat quirky charm, I think. The key to crocheting a "square" granny is to turn your work after each round. This means working on the 'wrong' side every other round. Not only does it prevent your granny square ending up leaning to one side, it also means that your blanket is reversible. Rather stubbornly, I started mine not turning, but noticed the "lean" after only ten rounds. I very swiftly started anew, and this time turned my work after every row. All the twisting, twirling and turning was avoided. I like seeing the perfectly straight sides on my Giant Granny Square!

Finished Size

Blanket measures about
47" (120 cm) square
(excluding tassels)

WHAT YOU'LL NEED

✱ **DMC Natura Just Cotton XL**
Various Colors – 22 balls in total

Designer's Note: *I used the following colors: #10 (2 balls), #81 (2 balls), #92, #07, #83, #71, #11, #12, #03 (2 balls), #05, #51, #06 (2 balls), #43, #32, #111, #73, #42, #09*

Hook: Size N/15 (10 mm)

Yarn Needle

PATTERN NOTES

✱ Turn your work after each round (to work in wrong side of stitches on previous round)

✱ Fasten off after each color change

✱ Weave in all ends as you go

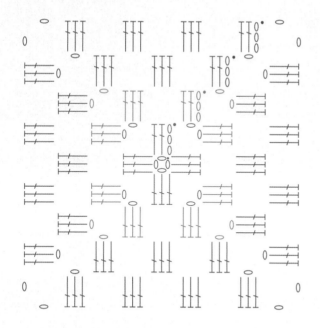

⬯ **ch** - chain

● **ss** - slip stitch

⊤ **dc** - double crochet

GIANT GRANNY

ROUND 1: Starting with any color, ch 4, join with sl st to first ch to form a ring (or start with a Magic Ring - see Techniques), ch 3 (counts as first dc, now and throughout), 2 dc in ring, ch 2, *3 dc in ring, ch 2; rep from * twice more; join with sl st to first dc (3rd ch of beg ch-3). Fasten off.

ROUND 2: Turn, with next color, join with sl st to any ch-2 sp, ch 3, 2dc in same sp, *skip next 3 dc, (3 dc, ch 2, 3 dc) in next ch-2 sp; rep from * twice more, skip next 3 dc, 3 dc in same first ch-2 sp (as ch-3 & 2 dc), ch 2; join with sl st to first dc. Fasten off.

Designer's Tip: *When starting with a new color, instead of joining and working a ch-3 for the first dc, use a standing stitch with the new color (see Techniques).*

ROUND 3: Turn, with next color, join with sl st to any corner ch-2 sp, ch 3, 2 dc in same sp, skip next 3 dc, 3 dc in sp between dc-groups, *skip next 3 dc, (3 dc, ch 2, 3 dc) in next ch-2 sp, skip next 3 dc, 3 dc in sp between dc-groups; rep from * twice more, skip next 3 dc, 3 dc in same first ch-2 sp; ch 2; join with sl st to first dc. Fasten off.

Designer's Tip: *When joining the next color on a new round, start in a different corner each time (so that the joins do not lie on a diagonal – they are randomly placed).*

ROUND 4: Turn, with next color, join with sl st to any corner ch-2 sp, ch 3, 2 dc in same sp, work 3 dc in each sp around, working (3 dc, ch 2, 3 dc) in each corner ch-2 sp, ending with 3 dc in same first corner ch-2 sp, ch 2; join with sl st to first dc. Fasten off.

Designer's Tip: *From here on, you work (3 dc, ch 2, 3 dc) in each corner, and 3 dc between each group of 3 dc-sts.*

ROUNDS 5-31 (Or Desired Size): Rep Rnd 4, changing color each round.

Designer's Hint: *The Round number is the same number of dc-groups between two corner ch-2 spaces! It's a good idea to keep checking that you have the same number of dc-groups along all four sides – to keep everything square.*

TASSELS

Cut strands of yarn, about 16" (40 cm) long, in all the colors you used (you'll need about 512 strands.)

*Holding 4 different colored strands together, fold in half.

Working in last round, insert hook from back to front through any space between dc-groups.

Place the folded ends on hook and pull them halfway through to form a loop. Place all eight ends on the hook and pull them through the loop. Tug to tighten.

Repeat from * around, putting a tassel in each space between dc-groups and in each corner ch-2 sp.

Granny Square Cardigan "Marie"

Skill Level
**

Can you fall in love with a piece of crochet? It must be so, because I fell in love - head over heels - with this cardigan! The minute I finished sewing in the last yarn end and tried it on... Oh, my! My heart was aflutter. What a joy it is to wear - so nice and soft and warm, yet not too heavy. I even love how it looks on me. So yes, all sorts of love and happiness! I've named this design, in honor of my dear grandmother, "Marie". If you're not the crochet-cardigan kind of person, or feel somewhat intimidated to try a challenging project like this, you can always use these colorful granny squares to make a beautiful blanket.

Finished Size

To fit average women with
bust measurements
40" - 46" (102 cm - 117 cm)

Length from shoulder
(including border) – 40" (101 cm)

Width from side to side
(under armholes) – 24 ½" (62 cm)

Width across bottom – Front
corner to Front corner –
51 ¼" (130 cm) (incl. border)

Each Granny Square = about
4" (10 cm) square

WHAT YOU'LL NEED

✴ **DMC Natura Just Cotton**
Main Color - MC (Black N11) – 8 balls
Selection of Various Colors – about 1-2 balls each

Designer's Note: I used 1 ball each of: N02, N05, N09, N13, N14, N23, N26, N32, N35, N43, N47, N51, N54, N59, N80, N81, N83, N85; and 2 balls each of N61 and N64.

Hook: Size E-4 (3.5 mm)

Yarn Needle

PATTERN NOTES

✴ Do not turn after each round/row

✴ Fasten off after each color change

✴ Weave in all ends as you go

SPECIAL STITCHES

hdc2tog: Yarn over, insert hook in stitch of space indicated and pull up a loop (3 loops on hook), (do not yarn over) insert hook in next stitch or space and pull up a loop (4 loops on hook), yarn over and draw through all four loops on hook.

hdc3tog: Yarn over, insert hook in stitch of space indicated and pull up a loop (3 loops on hook), *(do not yarn over) insert hook in next stitch or space and pull up a loop; rep from * once more (5 loops on hook), yarn over and draw through all five loops on hook.

Designer's Note: To go up or down sizes you can easily adjust the pattern by adding or leaving out 1 (or more) rows on your granny squares, or even adjust the rows of granny squares needed. Making a swatch and measuring is key here; I used an old cardigan to get my measurements right!

GRANNY SQUARE – Make 138

ROUND 1: (Right Side) Using any color, ch 4, join with sl st to first ch to form a ring (or start with a Magic Ring - see Techniques), ch 5 (counts as first dc & ch-2, now and throughout), *3 dc in ring, ch 2; rep from * twice more, 2 dc in ring; join with sl st to first dc (3rd ch of beg ch-5). (4 groups of 3-dc each & 4 corner ch-2 sps) Fasten off.

ROUND 2: With right side facing, join new color with sl st to any corner ch-2 sp, ch 5, 3 dc in same sp, *(3 dc, ch 2, 3 dc) in next ch-2 sp; rep from * around, ending with 2 dc in same first corner ch-2 sp; join with sl st to first dc. (8 groups of 3-dc each & 4 corner ch-2 sps) Fasten off.

Designer's Tip: When starting with a new color, instead of joining and working a ch-3 for the first dc, use a standing stitch with the new color (see Techniques).

ROUND 3: With right side facing, join next new color with sl st to any corner ch-2 sp, ch 5, 3 dc in same sp, 3 dc in sp between next two 3-dc groups, *(3 dc, ch 2, 3 dc) in next ch-2 sp, 3 dc in sp between next two 3-dc groups; rep from * around, ending with 2 dc in same first corner ch-2 sp; join with sl st to first dc. (12 groups of 3-dc each & 4 corner ch-2 sps) Fasten off.

ROUND 4: With right side facing, join next new color with sl st to any ch-2 corner, ch 5, 3 dc in same sp, [3 dc in next sp between groups] across to next corner, *(3 dc, ch 2, 3 dc) in next ch-2 sp, [3 dc in next sp between groups] across to next corner; rep from * around, ending with 2 dc in same first corner ch-2 sp; join with sl st to first dc. (16 groups of 3-dc each & 4 corner ch-2 sps) Fasten off.

ROUND 5: Rep Rnd 4. (20 groups of 3-dc each & 4 corner ch-2 sps) Fasten off.

Designer's Tip: I stopped after Round 5, until I had enough squares and then followed the layout diagrams, using the join-as-you-go method (see Techniques) for Round 6.

ROUND 6: With right side facing, using MC, repeat Rnd 4. (24 groups of 3-dc each & 4 corner ch-2 sps) Fasten off MC.

ROUND 6 (JOIN-AS-YOU-GO): Rep Rnd 6 up to the corner before the joining side(s). Across each joining side, work as follow:

3 dc in corner ch-2 sp, ch 1, working in previous Motif, sl st in corresponding corner ch-2 sp, ch 1, working in current Motif, 3 dc in same corner ch-2 sp, *working in previous Motif, sl st in next corresponding sp between dc-groups, working on current Motif, 3 dc in next sp between groups; rep from * across to next corner, 3 dc in corner ch-2 sp, ch 1, working in previous Motif, sl st in corresponding corner ch-2 sp, ch 1, working in current Motif, 3 dc in same corner ch-2 sp.

Continue with Round 6 as established; join with sl st to first dc. Fasten off MC.

GRANNY TRIANGLE – Make 6

ROW 1: (Right Side) Using any color, ch 4, join with sl st to first ch to form a ring (or start with a Magic Ring - see Techniqes), ch 3 (counts as first dc, now and throughout), 2 dc in ring, ch 2, 3 dc in ring. (2 groups of 3-dc each & 1 corner ch-2 sp) Fasten off.

ROW 2: With right side facing, join new color with sl st to first dc (3rd ch of ch-3), ch 3, 2 dc in same st, (3 dc, ch 2, 3 dc) in next ch-2 sp, skip next 2 dc, 3 dc in last dc. (4 groups of 3-dc each & 1 corner ch-2 sp) Fasten off.

ROWS 3-5: With right side facing, join new color with sl st to first dc (3rd ch of ch-3), ch 3, 2 dc in same st, [3 dc in sp between dc-groups] across to corner, (3 dc, ch 2, 3 dc) in next ch-2 sp, [3 dc in sp between dc-groups] across, ending with 3 dc in last dc. At the end of Row 5 there are (10 groups of 3-dc each & 1 corner ch-2 sp) Fasten off.

Designer's Tip: I stopped after each Row 5, and then used join-as-you-go (see Techniques) for Round 6.

ROUND 6: (Worked all the way around the Triangle) With right side facing, jjoin MC with sl st to first dc (3rd ch of ch-3), ch 3, (2 dc, ch 2, 3 dc) in same ch 3, [3 dc in sp between dc-groups] across to corner, (3 dc, ch 2, 3 dc) in next ch-2 sp, [3 dc in sp between dc-groups] across, ending with (3 dc, ch 2, 3 dc) in last dc, working in sides of rows at the base of sts, 2 dc in each of next 4 rows, 2 dc in starting ring, 2 dc in each of next 4 rows; join with sl st to first dc (3rd ch of beg ch-3). (14 groups of 3-dc each, 9 groups of 2 dc each & 3 corner ch-2 sps) Fasten off MC.

Designer's Note: For-Join-As-You-Go, you repeat the Granny Square's Round 6 (Join-As-You-Go) along all the joining sides.

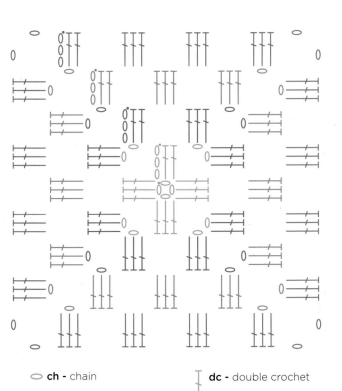

⬭ **ch -** chain

• **ss -** slip stitch

⊤ **dc -** double crochet

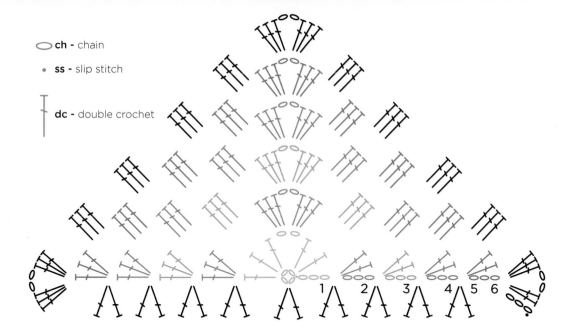

- ⬭ **ch** - chain
- • **ss** - slip stitch
- **dc** - double crochet

ASSEMBLY OF CARDIGAN

Designer's Note: *You can join the granny squares and triangles using any method you prefer. You can sew or crochet the seams together using either slip stitches or single crochet (on either the right or the wrong side – depending on what you like) or you can do like me and "join-as-you-go".*

Following the layout diagrams, with right sides facing:

1) Make four Sleeves, each using 8 Granny Squares, and join together in a 4 x 2 grid.

2) For the Back, join 54 Granny Squares (6 squares wide by 9 squares long) and attach 2 Sleeves and 2 Granny Triangles at underarm.

3) For each Front, join 26 Granny Squares (3 squares wide by 9 squares long, except for the top corner, where a Triangle goes) and attach Sleeves and underarm Triangles.

4) Join the Fronts to the Back along the side seams, underarms and shoulders.

Designer's Note: *It goes without saying that you can make your cardigan as long or short (or as wide) as you want. I wanted mine rather long, and so I used 9 granny squares.*

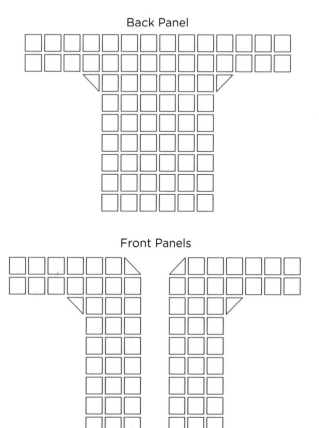

Back Panel

Front Panels

BORDER

ROUND 1: With right side of cardigan facing, join MC with sl st to any st along the bottom, near the side seam, ch 2, hdc in same st, hdc in each st around, working hdc2tog (see Special Stitches) at every junction of 2 Granny Squares (using corner ch-2 sp of each Square), hdc3tog (see Special Stitches) at the Front/Back junctions (using corner ch-2 sp of 3 squares), and working 5 hdc in each bottom Front corner ch-2 sp; join with sl st to first hdc. Fasten off MC.

Designer's Note: You can finish off your cardigan after Round 1 of the border. I prefer the colorful edging that Rounds 2-5 add to the overall look of the cardigan.

ROUND 2: With right side facing, with new color, join with sc (see Techniques) to any hdc, ch 2, *skip next 2 hdc, sc in next hdc, ch 2; working [(sc, ch 2, sc) in center hdc, ch 2] on each Front corner, and [skip next hdc, sc in next hdc3tog, ch 2] on each neckline corner; rep from * around, join with sl st to first sc. Fasten off color.

ROUND 3: With right side facing, join MC with sl st to any ch-2 sp, *3 hdc in next ch-2 sp; rep from * around, working [(2 hdc, ch 2, 2 hdc) in corner ch-2 sps] on each Front; join with sl st to first hdc. Fasten off MC.

ROUND 4: With right side facing, with next new color, join with sc to any center hdc (of 3-hdc group), ch 2, *skip next 2 hdc, sc in next (center) hdc, ch 2; rep from * around, working [skip next hdc, sc in next hdc, ch 2, sc in corner ch-2 sp, ch 2, sc in next hdc, ch 2] in each Front corner; join with sl st to first sc. Fasten off color.

ROUND 5: With right side facing, using MC, join with sc to any sc, *2 sc in next ch-2 sp, sc in next sc; rep from * around; join with sl st to first sc. Fasten off MC.

FINISHING

Lightly steam block.

Colorful Cushion Roll "Lenize"

Skill Level
*

A long time ago I made a Cushion Roll just like this and never wrote out the pattern. An omission I've now taken care of! The new Colorful Cushion Roll "Lenize" is a fun and relatively easy pattern. If you're a beginner and have mastered the granny square, this is the perfect next-step-up project. I hope you'll love crocheting it as much as I did!

Finished Size

Cushion Roll about 17 ½"
(45 cm) long with a 6"
(15 cm) diameter

Each Motif measures 6"
(15 cm) square

WHAT YOU'LL NEED

✻ DMC Natura Just Cotton Medium
Selection of Various Colors – about 1 ball each

Designer's Note: *I used the following colors - #02, #03, #05, #09, #12, #41, #44, #77, #99, #109, #126, #134, #177, #198, #444 & #700*

Hooks:

Size I-9 (5.50 mm) for Motifs

Size H-8 (5.00 mm) for the striped ends

Yarn Needle

Bolster Pillow Form

PATTERN NOTES

✻ Do not turn after each round

✻ Fasten off after each color change

✻ Weave in all ends as you go

SPECIAL STITCHES

Cluster (dc2tog): *Yarn over hook, insert hook in next st or sp indicated and pull up a loop, yarn over and draw through 2 loops on hook* (2 loops on hook), rep from * to * once (3 loops on hook), yarn over, draw through all 3 loops (cluster made).

MOTIF – Make 9

ROUND 1: (Right Side) Using any color, ch 8, join with sl st to first ch to form a ring (or start with a Magic Ring - see Techniques), ch 4 (counts as first dc & ch-1), *dc in ring, ch 1; rep from * 14 times more; join with sl st to first dc (3rd ch of beg ch-4). (16 dc & 16 ch-1 sps) Fasten off.

ROUND 2: With right side facing, join new color with sl st to any ch-1 sp, ch 5 (counts as first dc & ch-2, now and throughout), *dc in next ch-1 sp, ch 2; rep from * around; join with sl st to first dc. (16 dc & 16 ch-2 sps) Fasten off.

Designer's Tip: *When starting with a new color, instead of joining and working a ch-3 for the first dc, use a standing stitch with the new color (see Techniques).*

ROUND 3: With right side facing, using next color, join with sc (see Techniques) to any ch-2 sp, *(sc, 3 hdc, sc) in next ch-2 sp, sc in next ch-2 sp, (2 hdc, dc, ch 2, dc, 2 hdc) in next ch-2 sp (corner made)**, sc in next ch-2 sp; rep from * around, ending at ** on final repeat; join with sl st to first sc. (16 sc, 28 hdc, 8 dc & 4 ch-2 sps) Fasten off.

ROUND 4: With right side facing, join next new color with sl st to any corner ch-2 sp, ch 5, dc in same sp (corner made), *ch 2, skip next 3 sts, dc in next sc, ch 2, skip next 2 sts, sc in next (center) hdc, ch 2, skip next 2 sts, dc in next sc, skip next 3 sts**, (dc, ch 2, dc) in next corner ch-2 sp; rep from * around, ending at ** on final repeat; join with sl st to first dc (3rd ch of beg ch-5). (16 dc, 4 sc & 20 ch-2 sps)

ROUND 5: Ch 3 (counts as first dc), *(2 dc, 2 tr, 2 dc) in next ch-2 sp (corner made), [dc in next dc, 2 dc in next ch-2 sp] twice, dc in next sc, [2 dc in next ch-2 sp, dc in next dc] twice; rep from * around, omitting last dc on final repeat; join with sl st to first dc (3rd ch of beg ch-3). (68 dc & 8 tr) Fasten off.

Designer's Note: *Make sure to work a dc in the first dc after each corner. It's hiding a bit under the corner stitches.*

ASSEMBLY OF CUSHION ROLL

With wrong sides of all Motifs facing, using a length of yarn and yarn needle, join the motifs together in a 3 x 3 grid, by whip-stitching through the outer loops only. Then sew the top and bottom together, creating a cylinder (tube).

Designer's Tip: *Make three strips of three motifs each, then sew the strips together to form the tube.*

STRIPED ENDS

ROUND 1: (Right Side) Using the smaller hook, working around the tube opening, join next color (#134) with sl st to 2nd tr in any corner, ch 3, *dc in each of next 17 dc, dc in next tr, dc2tog (using next tr on current motif and 1st corner tr on next motif)**, dc in next tr; rep from * around, ending at ** on final repeat; join with sl st to first dc (3rd ch of beg ch-3). (60 dc) Fasten off.

ROUND 2: With right side facing, join next color (#700) with sl st in sp between any 2 dc, ch 3, working in sps between sts only, dc in each of next 2 sps, *dc2tog (using next 2 sps), dc in each of next 3 sps; rep from * around, ending with dc2tog; join with sl st to first dc. (48 dc) Fasten off.

ROUND 3: With right side facing, join next color (#09) with sl st in sp between any 2 dc, ch 3, working in sps between sts only, dc in next st, *dc2tog (using next 2 sps), dc in each of next 2 sps; rep from * around, ending with dc2tog; join with sl st to first dc. (36 dc) Fasten off.

ROUND 4: With right side facing, join next color (#444) with sl st in sp between any 2 dc, ch 3, working in sps between sts only, *dc in next sp; rep from * around; join with sl st to first dc. (36 dc) Fasten off.

ROUNDS 5-7: Rep Round 4 (Colors used #126, #198 & #77) Rep Rounds 1-7 on opposite end.

TIES – Make 2

Using any color and smaller hook, ch 60. Fasten off.

Weave Ties through last round of both Striped Ends and tie in a bow.

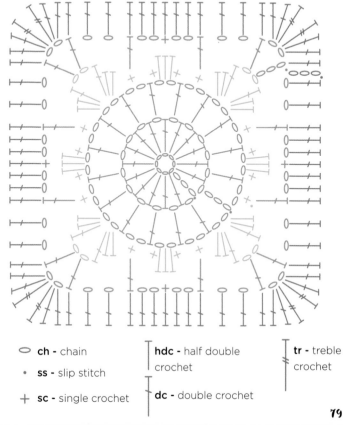

⬭ **ch -** chain	**hdc -** half double crochet	**tr -** treble crochet
ss - slip stitch		
+ sc - single crochet	**dc -** double crochet	

Hexagon Blanket "Inez"

Skill Level
★★★

There's something special about a hexagon, I think, particularly when it's crocheted. After returning to crochet in 2010, one of the first projects I made was a hexagon blanket. Looking at the original blanket now, one can see that at the time I still needed a lot to learn about crochet basics. Even though it's far from perfect, I love it all the same. Two of my crochet crushes come together in this design: the hexagon shape and textured stitching. I've used puff stitches in the last round (using join-as-you-go) to "frame" each hexagon. The join-as-you-go method is the only way to get the "hexies-with-puffs" nicely joined, but this is definitely a challenge. However, with a bit of concentration and focus, you'll master the technique soon enough, and will be joining your "hexies" in a jiffy. Another plus of this puff-round, is that no additional border is needed. However, you can easily omit the last round and sew or crochet your 4-round hexagons and half hexagons together without the puff-edge. I couldn't resist trying this pattern using a single color as well, to see the effect, and I love how the Blue Blanket turned out!

Finished Size

Colorful Blanket measures
31 ½" (80 cm) wide and
43 ½" (110 cm) long

Each Colorful Motif is 7"
(18 cm) diameter

Blue Blanket measures 31 ½" (80
cm) wide and 47" (120 cm) long

Each Blue Motif is 9 ½"
(24 cm) diameter

WHAT YOU'LL NEED

Yarn Needle

For Colorful Blanket

❋ **DMC Natura Just Cotton Medium**

Color A (#99) – 2 balls
Color B (#41) – 2 balls
Color C (#77) – 4 balls
Color D (#134) – 4 balls
Color E (#444) – 5 balls

Hook: Size J-10 (6 mm)

For Blue Blanket

❋ **DMC Natura Just Cotton XL**

Main Color - MC (#73 Aqua) - 11 balls

Hook: Size L-11 (8 mm)

PATTERN NOTES

❋ Do not turn after each round/row

❋ Fasten off after each color change

❋ Weave in all ends as you go

❋ The pattern is written for the Colorful Blanket. For the Blue Blanket, do not fasten off and change colors

SPECIAL STITCHES

Bobble Stitch (bob): Yarn over hook, insert hook in st or sp indicated and pull up a loop, yarn over and draw through 2 loops on hook (2 loops on hook). Yarn over and insert hook in same stich and pull up a loop (4 loops on hook), yarn over draw through 2 loops on hook (3 loops remain), yarn over, draw through remaining 3 loops (bobble made).

Cluster (dc2tog): *Yarn over hook, insert hook in next st or sp indicated and pull up a loop, yarn over and draw through 2 loops on hook* (2 loops on hook), rep from * to * once (3 loops on hook), yarn over, draw through all 3 loops (cluster made).

Cluster (dc3tog): *Yarn over hook, insert hook in next st or sp indicated and pull up a loop, yarn over and draw through 2 loops on hook* (2 loops on hook), rep from * to * twice (4 loops on hook), yarn over, draw through all 4 loops (cluster made).

Puff Stitch (puff): In same st or sp indicated, [yo hook, insert hook, pull up a loop (to height of hdc)] 3 times (7 loops on hook), yo and draw through all 7 loops on the hook, ch 1 (to lock) (puff stitch made).

HEXAGON – Make 27 (Make 18 for Blue Blanket)

ROUND 1: (Right Side) Using Color A, ch 6; join with sl st to first ch to form a ring (or start with a Magic Ring - see Techniques); ch 3 (counts as first dc, now and throughout), 17 dc in ring; join with sl st to first dc (3rd ch of beg ch-3). (18 dc) Fasten off Color A.

ROUND 2: With right side facing, join Color B with sl st to any dc, ch 2, dc in same st (first bobble made), ch 1, *bob (see Special Stitches) in next dc, ch 1; rep from * around; join with sl st to first dc. (18 bobbles & 18 ch-1 sps) Fasten off Color B.

ROUND 3: With right side facing, join Color C with sl st to top of any bobble, ch 2, dc2tog (using next ch-1 sp and next bobble – first cluster made – see Special Stitches), ch 2, *dc3tog (using same bobble, next ch-1 sp and next bobble – see Special Stitches), ch 2; rep from * around; join with sl st to first cluster. (18 clusters & 18 ch-2 sps) Fasten off Color C.

Designer's Tip: The 1st dc of each cluster is worked in the same st as the 3rd dc of the previous cluster.

ROUND 4: With right side facing, join Color D with sl st to any ch-2 sp, ch 3, 2 dc in same sp, *5 dc in next ch-2 sp (corner made), 3 dc in each of next 2 ch-2 sps; rep from * around, omitting last 3 dc on final repeat; join with sl st to first dc. (6 dc between each 5-dc corner) Fasten off.

Designer's Tips: *When starting with a new color, instead of joining and working a ch-3 for the first dc, use a standing stitch with the new color (see Techniques).*

Do not forget to close each Puff Stitch with a ch 1 to lock!

ROUND 5: With right side facing, join Color E with sl st to center dc of any 5-dc corner, ch 2, puff (see Special Stitches) in same st, *[ch 1, skip next 2 dc, sl st in next dc, puff in same dc] 3 times, ch 1, skip next dc**, sl st in next dc (center dc of 5-dc group), puff in same dc; rep from * around, ending at ** on final repeat; join with sl st to base of first puff (same dc as joining). (24 puffs – 4 puffs along each side - & 24 ch-1 sps) Fasten off Color E.

Designer's Hint: *After the first Hexagon, I work all the other hexagons up to Round 4. Once they're all done, I work the join-as-you-go Round 5.*

For Remaining Hexagons

ROUND 5 (Joining Round): Following the layout diagram, rep Round 5, but on the side/s that are to be joined, starting at any corner, holding the previous Hexagon behind (right sides facing, wrong sides together), work as follows:

Puff in first dc of corner 5-dc group, working on Previous Hexagon, sl st in corresponding ch-1 sp (between the 2 corner puffs), working on Current Hexagon, skip next dc, sl st in next (center) dc, puff in same dc, *working in Previous Hexagon, sl st in next ch-1 sp, working on Current Hexagon, skip next 2 dc, sl st in next dc, puff in same st; rep from * and end with a sl st in the ch-1 sp of the next corner of the Previous Hexagon (one side joined - 5 joins); continue with Round 5 as established. At the end of the round, fasten off.

Designer's Tip: *Start by joining one side of each Hexagon to form a strip (Hexagons 1-5), then continue with the next number, joining either one, two or three sides as shown in the layout diagram.*

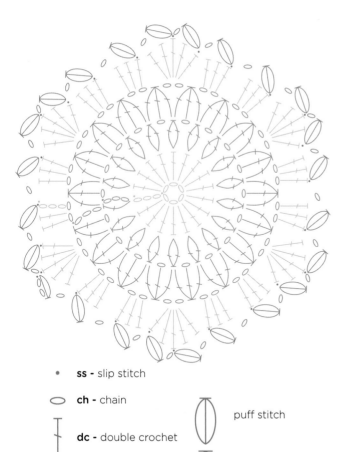

- • **ss -** slip stitch
- ⬭ **ch -** chain
- ⊢ **dc -** double crochet
- **2-dc bobble**
- **puff stitch**
- **3-dc cluster**

Designer's Note: *If you're like me, you want to fill in the big gaps around the blanket. That's what the half- hexagons are for.*

HALF-HEXAGON (Optional) Make 6 (Make 4 for Blue Blanket)

ROW 1: (Right Side) Using Color A, ch 4; join with sl st to first ch to form a ring (or start with a Magic Ring - see Techniques); ch 3 (counts as first dc, now and throughout), 6 dc in ring; DO NOT JOIN. (7 dc) Fasten off Color A.

ROW 2: With right side facing, join Color B with sl st to first dc (3rd ch of beg ch-3), ch 4 (counts as first dc & ch 1), *bob in sp between 2 dc, ch 1; rep from * 5 times, ending with dc in last dc. (2 dc, 6 bobbles & 7 ch-1 sps) Fasten off Color B.

ROW 3: With right side facing, join Color C with sl st to first dc, ch 5 (counts as first dc & ch-2), dc3tog (using same first dc, next ch-1 sp and next bobble – first cluster made), ch 2, *dc3tog (using same bobble, next ch-1 sp and next bobble), ch 2; rep from * 4 times, dc3tog (using same bobble, next ch-1 sp and last dc), ch 2, dc in same last dc. (2 dc, 7 clusters & 8 ch-2 sps) Fasten off Color C.

ROW 4: With right side facing, join Color D with sl st to first dc, ch 3, 2 dc in next ch-2 sp, 3 dc in each of next 2 ch-2 sps, 5 dc in next ch-2 sp, 3 dc in top of next (center) cluster, 5 dc in next ch-2 sp, 3 dc in each of next 2 ch-2 sps, 2 dc in last ch-2 sp, dc in last dc. (31 dc) Fasten off Color D.

ROUND 5: With right side facing, join Color E with sl st to last dc made, ch 2, puff in same st, ch 1, working in sides of rows (along straight edge), *sl st in top of next dc, puff in same dc, ch 1*; rep from * to * three times, sl st in center ring, puff in same sp, ch 1; rep from * to * 3 times, working in Row 4, sl st in first dc, puff in same dc, [ch 1, skip next 2 dc, sl st in next dc (first dc of 3-dc-group), puff in same dc] 2 times, ch 1, skip next 2 dc, sl st in next dc (first dc of 5-dc-group), puff in same dc (first side complete), ch 1, skip next dc, sl st in next dc (center dc of 5-dc-group), puff in same dc, [ch 1, skip next 2 dc, sl st in next dc, puff in same dc] 2 times, ch 1, skip next dc, sl st in next dc (center of 5-dc-group), puff in same dc (second side complete), [ch 1, skip next 2 dc, sl st in next dc, puff in same dc] 3 times, skip next dc, sl st in next dc (last dc of

ASSEMBLING THE BLANKET

Whether you're using the "join-as-you-go method, or sewing or crocheting your hexagons together, this is the layout diagram to follow.

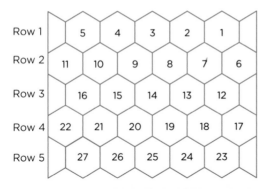

Row 4), puff in same dc, join with sl st to base of first puff (same dc as joining - third side complete). (20 puffs - 8 along the straight edge & 4 along the other three sides - & 20 ch-1 sps) Fasten off Color E.

Designer's Notes: *The Half Hexagons are joined on the short sides, not along the 8-puff straight edge.*

When you're joining a half hex on all three sides, the very last slip stitch will have to be made in the corner of the adjoining full hex, between 2 corner puffs.

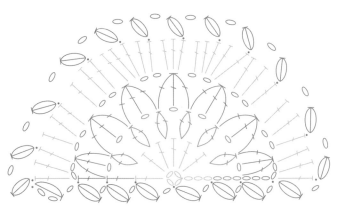

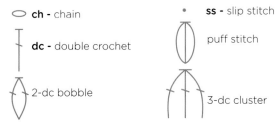

⬯ **ch -** chain	• **ss -** slip stitch
╪ **dc -** double crochet	puff stitch
⬙ 2-dc bobble	3-dc cluster

Half Hexagon - Join-As-You-Go:

ROUND 5: Following the layout diagram, rep Round 5 across the straight edge of the Half-Hexagon and up to the side(s) that are to be joined, holding the Hexagon behind (right sides facing - wrong sides together), work each joining side as follows:

After the last puff of the unjoined side is complete, working in Hexagon, sl st in corresponding ch-1 sp (between 2 corner puffs), working in Row 4 of Half-Hexagon, sl st in first dc, puff in same dc, working in Hexagon, sl st in corresponding ch-1 sp, [working in Half-Hexagon, skip next 2 dc, sl st in next dc (first dc of 3-dc-group), puff in same dc, working in Hexagon, sl st in corresponding ch-1 sp] 2 times, working in Half Hexagon, skip next 2 dc, sl st in next dc (first dc of 5-dc-group), puff in same dc, working in Hexagon, sl st in corresponding corner ch-1 sp (one side joined - 5 joins), working in Half-Hexagon, skip next dc, sl st in next dc (center of 5-dc-group), puff in same dc, working in Hexagon, sl st in corresponding ch-1 sp, working in Half-Hexagon, skip next 2 dc, sl st in next dc (first of 3-dc group), puff in same dc, working in Hexagon, sl st in corresponding ch-1 sp, working in Half-Hexagon, skip next 2 dc, sl st in next dc (first dc of 5-dc-group), puff in same dc, working in Hexagon, sl st in corresponding ch-1 sp, working in Half-Hexagon, skip next dc, sl st in next dc (center dc of 5-dc-group), puff in same dc, working in Hexagon, sl st in corresponding corner ch-1 sp (second side joined), [working in Half-Hexagon, skip next 2 dc, sl st in next dc (first dc of 3-dc-group), puff in same dc, working in Hexagon, sl st in corresponding ch-1 sp], 3 times, working in Half-Hexagon, skip next dc, sl st in next dc (last dc of Row 4), puff in same dc, working in Hexagon, sl st in corresponding ch-1 corner (between 2 corner puffs). Fasten off.

Hexagon Shawl "Ursula"

Skill Level
✱ ✱

The "Sunshine Blanket" made me extra aware of how much I love working on a crochet project when suddenly a whole new design appears after you've joined a few crocheted motifs together. The hexagons used in this shawl did exactly that. It seems as if the borders of every single motif disappear and all the hexagons blend together into this bigger motif, as do the lines of the puff stitches.

Needless to say, I love this hexagon shawl!

Finished Size

Shawl (trapezium-shaped)
measures:
61" (155 cm) along the top;
39 ½" (100 cm) along the
bottom; and 29 ½"
(75 cm) along each side.

Each Motif is about 5 ½"
(14 cm) from side
to side

WHAT YOU'LL NEED

✱ **DMC Woolly**

Main Color (#041) – 9 balls

Hooks:
Size K-10½ (6.5 mm) – for Hexagons
Size I-9 (5.5 mm) – for Border

Yarn Needle

PATTERN NOTES

✱ Do not turn after each round

✱ Weave in all ends as you go

SPECIAL STITCHES

Puff Stitch (puff): In same st or sp indicated, [yo hook, insert hook, pull up a loop (to height of hdc)] 4 times (9 loops on hook), yo and draw through all 9 loops on the hook, ch 1 (to lock) (puff Stitch made).

Note: *When working in a puff-stitch on the following row/round, you insert your hook under the locking chain-stitch.*

HEXAGON – Make 45

ROUND 1: (Right Side) Using larger hook, ch 4; join with sl st to first ch to form a ring (or start with a Magic Ring - see Techniques); ch 3 (counts as first dc, now and throughout), 11 dc in ring; join with sl st to first dc (3rd ch of beg ch-3). (12 dc)

Designer's Tip: *Do not forget to close each Puff Stitch with a ch 1 to lock!*

ROUND 2: Ch 3, (puff (see Special Stitches), dc) in same st as joining, *ch 2, skip next dc**, (dc, puff, dc) in next dc; rep from * around, ending at ** on final repeat; join with sl st to first dc. (12 dc, 6 puffs & 6 ch-2 sps)

ROUND 3: Ch 3, dc in same st as joining, *puff in top of next puff, 2 dc in next dc, ch 2, skip next ch-2 sp**, 2 dc in next dc; rep from * around, ending at ** on final repeat; join with sl st to first dc. (24 dc, 6 puffs & 6 ch-2 sps)

ROUND 4: Ch 3, dc in same st as joining, *dc in next dc, puff in top of next puff, dc in next dc, 2 dc in next dc, ch 2, skip next ch-2 sp**, 2 dc in next dc; rep from * around, ending at ** on final repeat; join with sl st to first dc. (36 dc, 6 puffs & 6 ch-2 sps)

ROUND 5: Ch 3, dc in same st as joining, *dc in each of next 2 dc, puff in top of next puff, dc in each of next 2 dc, 2 dc in next dc, ch 2, skip next ch-2 sp**, 2 dc in next dc; rep from * around, ending at ** on final repeat; join with sl st to first dc. (48 dc, 6 puffs & 6 ch-2 sps) Fasten off.

Designer's Note: *My hexagons are all joined using the PLT (pull loop through - see Techniques) method, but you can just as easily sew or crochet them together. After completing the first hexagon (Rounds 1-5), all the remaining hexagons get joined on Round 5, either along one, two or three sides following the layout diagram.*

ROUND 5 - PLT Method (optional)

Following the diagram with numbered motifs, for the next Motif, rep Rnd 5 until the corner before you need to join.

First join the corner: Ch 1, working in previous Hexagon, sl st in corresponding ch-2 sp, ch 1 (corner is joined).

Now join each st across side, as follows: Make the loop a bit bigger and remove the hook. Insert the hook from front to back in next st on the same previous Hexagon, place loop back on hook and pull through st.

Following Rnd 5 instructions, work the next st (dc/puff) in the corresponding st on the current Hexagon.

Continue joining in each st across to the next corner and join the next corner as before. (One side joined)

Designer's Hint: *On some Hexagons, you'll be joining more than one side. Keep track of things by following the layout diagram and crossing off the blocks (on the diagram) of those you have finished and joined.*

JOINING THE HEXAGONS

Following the assembly diagram, sew or crochet all hexagons together following the numbers.

BORDER

After all 5 rows of Hexagons are joined (as shown in the diagram), using the smaller hook, join with sl st to any corner ch-2 sp, crab-st (see Techniques) in each st around, working 2 crab-sts in each corner ch-2 sp; join. Fasten off.

Once you have sewn in all the ends, gently steamblock Shawl "Ursula".

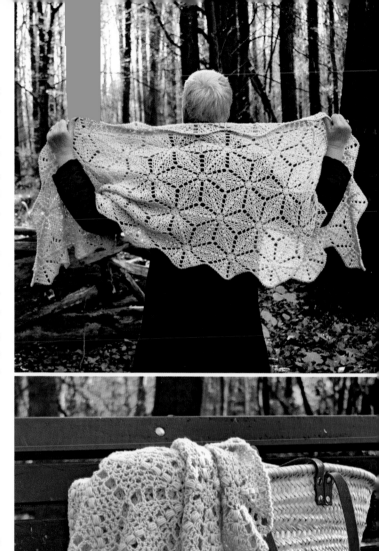

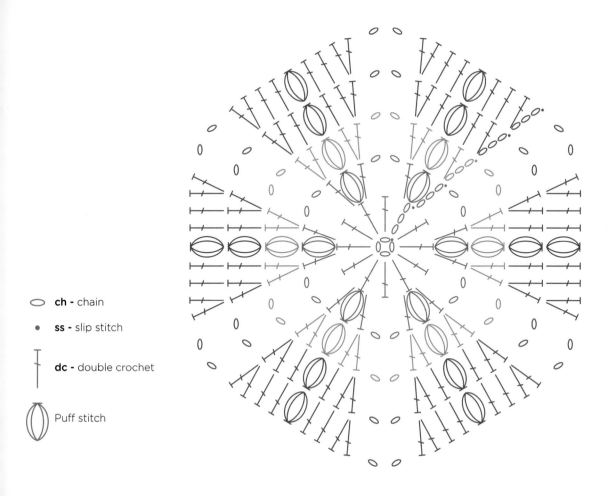

- ⬭ **ch -** chain
- ● **ss -** slip stitch
- ╪ **dc -** double crochet
- ⬯ Puff stitch

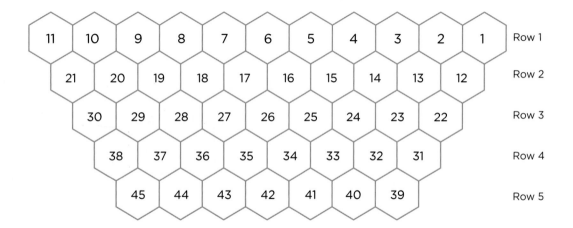

11	10	9	8	7	6	5	4	3	2	1	Row 1
21	20	19	18	17	16	15	14	13	12	Row 2
30	29	28	27	26	25	24	23	22	Row 3
38	37	36	35	34	33	32	31	Row 4
45	44	43	42	41	40	39	Row 5

Hybrid Blanket & Cushion "Lotte"

Skill Level
**

Tunisian crochet is a great technique, creating a thicker, one-sided fabric. The Tunisian Simple Stitch is relatively easy to learn, and creates an absolutely different look. As it is worked from the front only, you never turn your work. Generally one would use a long Tunisian crochet hook, but for this pattern, you might be able to fit all 12 stitches onto your normal crochet hook. In this Hybrid Blanket and Cushion I've combined Tunisian crochet (the heart of the Block) with regular crochet (the Block's border). While crocheting projects for this book I came to realize why I enjoy making cushion covers so much. They're fast to make, and yet another great opportunity to explore new color combinations using the same pattern. This is precisely what I did after having finished my Hybrid Blanket, resulting in this colorful Hybrid Cushion cover. To make the colors speak out even more I joined the Tunisian squares with black; I love a bit of drama in my crochet every once in a while.

Finished Size

Blanket measures
36" (90 cm) square

Cushion measures
18" (45 cm) square

Each Block
6" (15 cm) square

WHAT YOU'LL NEED

For the Blanket

❋ **DMC Natura Just Cotton Medium**
Main Color – MC - 10 balls
Color A – 5 balls

Designer's Note: *In the one blanket, I used Off-White (#03) for Color A and Petrol (#177) for the Main Color. In the other one, I liked the Grey (#12) for Color A together with the Purple (#126) for the Main Color*

For the Cushion

❋ **DMC Natura Just Cotton Medium**
Main Color – MC (#02 Black) - 2 balls
Color A - Various Colors – 1 ball each

Designer's Note: *I used #05, #09, #44, #77, #109, #126, #198, #444 & #700*

Pillow Form – 18" (45 cm) square

Fabric to cover pillow form

Needle and matching thread

Hooks:
Size J-10 (6 mm) Tunisian hook (if possible)
Size J-10 (6 mm) for Border

Yarn Needle

PATTERN NOTES

❋ Weave in all ends as you go

SPECIAL STITCHES

Single Crochet Decrease (sc2tog): Insert hook in next stitch and pull up a loop, (two loops on hook), insert hook in next stitch and pull up a loop (3 loops on hook), yarn over, draw through all three loops on hook (decrease made).

TUNISIAN BLOCK

Make 36 for Blanket/ Make 9 for Cushion

Designer's Note: *Each row in Tunisian Crochet consists of two 'passes' – a Forward Pass (picking up the loops) and a Return Pass (crocheting them off the hook).*

FIRST ROW: (Right Side) Using Color A and Tunisian hook (or normal a hook with a longish shaft), ch 12.

Forward Pass: Working in back ridge of chain (see Techniques) pick up loop in 2nd ch from hook, keeping loops on hook, pick up loop in each of next 10 chs. (12 lps on hook)

Return Pass: Ch 1, *yo, draw through 2 lps on hook; rep from * across to end (1 lp remains on hook).

Designer's Tip: *Generally, you start every Tunisian Return Pass with a chain one.*

SECOND ROW:

Designer's Tip: *Tug yarn gently before starting the Forward Pass. This eliminates having loose stitches along the right hand edge.*

Forward Pass: Insert hook from right to left under 2nd vertical bar of stitch (skip the first one, which is directly below the loop on your hook), yarn over hook and pull loop through (two loops on hook), keeping all loops on hook, *insert hook under next vertical bar and pull up a loop; rep from * across to last stitch (the ch-1 st of the Return Pass), insert hook through two loops of last st (the front lp and back ridge of the ch-st) and pick up loop. (12 lps on hook)

Return Pass: Ch 1, *yo, draw through 2 lps on hook; rep from * across to end.

Designer's Tip: *Working through two loops of the last (ch) stitch, gives a very neat edge. Looking at it, you should see a vertical row of 'v's. Having these 'v's is handy for when you're working the Border.*

THIRD TO TENTH ROW

Rep Forward Pass and Return Pass of Second Row.

At the end of the 10th Row, there are 10 rows of vertical loops visible on the right side of the fabric.

LAST ROW (Bind Off)

Forward Pass Only: *Insert hook from right to left under 2nd vertical bar and pick up lp, pulling it through the loop on hook (a slip stitch – leaving 1 lp on hook); rep from * across. No Return Pass.

At the end of the Row, fasten off Color A.

BLOCK BORDER

ROUND 1: With right side of Tunisian Block facing, using normal hook and MC, join with sc (see Techniques) in first st on last row (counts as first sc), sc in each of next 4 st, sc2tog (see Special Stitches), sc in each of next 4 sts (10 sc along top), ch 2 (corner made), working in sides of rows, skip st made in last forward pass/bind off row, sc in each of next 10 rows, ch 2 (next corner made); working in unused lps on other side of starting ch, sc in each of first 5 ch, sc2tog, sc in each of next 4 ch, ch 2 (next corner made), working in sides of rows, sc in each of next 10 rows, ch 2 (last corner made); join with sl st to first sc. (40 sc & 4 ch-2 sp)

ROUND 2: Ch 3 (counts as first dc, now and throughout), dc in each sc around, working (dc, ch 2, dc) in each corner ch-2 sp; join with sl st to first dc (3rd ch of beg ch-3). (48 dc & 4 ch-2 sps)

ROUND 3: Ch 3, *ch 1, skip next dc, dc in next dc; rep from * across to next corner, ch 1, (dc, ch 4, dc) in corner ch-2 sp; rep from * around, ending with ch-1; join with sl st to first dc. (32 dc, 28 ch-1 sps & 4 ch-4 sps) Fasten off MC.

Designer's Note: *If you choose to Join-As-You-Go, from the second block on, you will be using Round 3 as the joining round.*

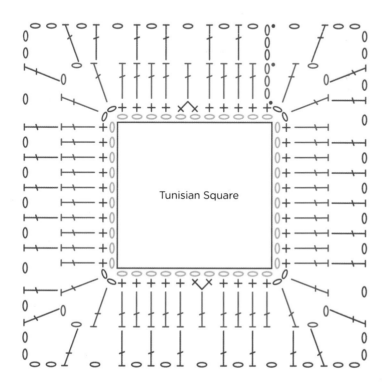

Tunisian Square

⬭	**ch -** chain
•	**ss -** slip stitch
+	**sc -** single crochet
⤬	**sc2tog**
⊤	**dc -** double crochet

JOINING OF BLOCKS

Designer's Hint: You might want to pay attention to the vertical Tunisian stitches in the Blocks, and line them up in the same direction when joining the borders.

Assemble the blocks in a 6 block by 6 block grid for the blanket, or a 3 by 3 block grid for the Cushion. Either sew or crochet the blocks together.

Designer's Note: I like the look of the flat Zipper Join (see Techniques) but prefer the ease of the Join-As-You-Go method.

ROUND 3 (Join-As-You-Go Alternative): Rep Rnd 3 up to the corner before side needing joining, ♥ dc in corner ch-2 sp, ch 2, working on previous Block, sl st in corresponding ch-4 corner, ch 2, working in current Block, dc in same corner ch-2 sp, *working in previous Block sl st in corresponding ch-1 sp, working in current Block, skip next dc, dc in next dc; rep from * across to next corner, ch 1, dc in corner ch-2 sp, ch 2, working in previous Block, sl st in corresponding ch-4 sp, ch 2, working on current Block, dc in same corner ch-2 sp, ch 1 ♥; rep from ♥ to ♥ for each side needing joining; continue with Round 3 above to complete round; join with sl st to first dc. Fasten off MC.

Designer's Hint: When joining more than 2 corners, the corner sl st goes into the side of the sl st previously made.

BORDER

ROUND 1: With right side facing, using MC and normal hook, join with sc to any corner, 3 sc in same corner, *sc in next dc, sc in next ch-sp; rep from * around, working 2 sc in first joined corner, sc in join, 2 sc in next joined corner (at each joining), and working 4 sc in each corner; join with sl st to first sc. Fasten off MC.

Designer's Note: This blanket and cushion will definitely benefit from a gentle steam blocking when finished.

FINISHING THE CUSHION

Make a fabric cover for the pillow form. Using needle and thread, sew the Cushion to the front of the cover.

"Merry-Go-Round" Granny Square Cushion

Skill Level
*

Playing around with the "corner-to-corner" stitches and technique was how this non-traditional granny square arose. You might not think so, but they're really not difficult to make, and most certainly qualify as a quick project. The colors I chose for my squares were inspired by the cute flowery fabric (roses, what else?) I found in my stash. I'm a bit in love with the pretty contrast... Modern looking squares paired with the romantic fabric.

Finished Size

Cushion Front measures 16" (40 cm) square

Each Block is 4" (10 cm) square

WHAT YOU'LL NEED

✱ **DMC Natura Just Cotton Medium**

Color A (#444) – 2 balls

Color B (#77) – 2 balls

Color C (#03) – 2 balls

Color D (#198) –2 balls

Color E (#44) – 1 ball

Color F (#134) – 1 ball

Designer's Note: The amounts given above are enough for 2 Fronts (or a Front and a Back)

Hook: Size J-10 (6 mm)

Yarn Needle

Pillow Form

Fabric for Pillow Form

Needle and matching thread

PATTERN NOTES

✱ Do not turn after each round

✱ Weave in all ends as you go

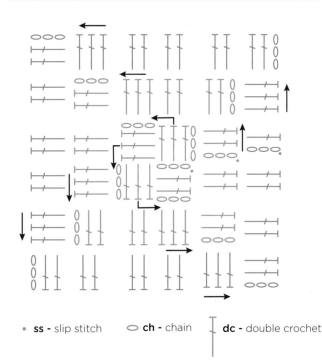

• **ss** - slip stitch ⬭ **ch** - chain │ **dc** - double crochet

BLOCKS – Make 16

ROUND 1: (Right Side) Using any color, ch 6, dc in 4th ch from hook, dc in each of next 2 ch, *ch 3, 3 dc over post of last dc made, rep from * once more, ch 3, 2 dc over post of last dc made; join with sl st to first skipped ch (4th ch of ch-6). (2 open dc & 1 ch-3 sp on each side.)

ROUND 2: Ch 3 (counts as first dc of round, now and throughout), 2 dc in next ch-3 sp, *ch 3, 2 dc over post of last dc made, dc in each of next 2 dc, 3 dc in next ch-3 sp; rep from * twice more, ch 3, 2 dc over post of last dc made, dc in each of next 2 dc; join with sl st to first dc (3rd ch of beg ch-3). (6 open dc & 1 ch-3 sp on each side.)

ROUND 3: Ch 3, dc in next dc, 3 dc in next ch-3 sp, *ch 3, 2 dc over post of last dc made, dc in each of next 6 dc, 3 dc in next ch-3 sp; rep from * twice more, ch 3, 2 dc over post of last dc made, dc in each of next 4 dc; join with sl st to first dc (3rd ch of beg ch-3). (10 open dc & 1 ch-3 sp) Fasten off.

ASSEMBLY OF CUSHION

With wrong sides facing, sew the Blocks together in a 4 block by 4 block grid.

Make a fabric cover for the pillow form. Using needle and thread, sew the Cushion to the front of the cover.

Designer's Hint: Make an identical Back with another 16 Blocks and sew the Back & Front together.

Puff Shawl "Mechelina"

Skill Level
**

If you want to be warm and cozy during cold spells, this shawl (made from utterly soft merino wool) is definitely the one to crochet. However, the same design worked up in a nice cotton yarn will be equally enjoyable to wear during chilly summer nights.

Finished Size

Triangular Puff Shawl
59" (150 cm) wide
and 35 ½" (90 cm) long
(excluding Border)

WHAT YOU'LL NEED

✳ DMC Woolly

Main Color – MC (#073) – 9 balls

Hook: Size K-10½ (6.5 mm)

Yarn Needle

PATTERN NOTES

✳ Weave in all ends as you go

SPECIAL STITCHES

Puff Stitch (puff): In same st or sp indicated, [yo hook, insert hook, pull up a loop (to height of hdc)] 4 times (9 loops on hook), yo and draw through all 9 loops on the hook, ch 1 (to lock) (puff stitch made).

Note: When working in a puff stitch on the following row/round, you insert your hook under the locking chain-stitch.

TRIANGLE SHAPED SHAWL

ROW 1: (Right Side) With MC, ch 4, (dc, ch 1, 2 dc) in 4th ch from hook (skipped chs count as first dc). (4 dc & 1 ch-1 sp)

ROW 2: Ch 4 (counts as first tr, now and throughout), turn, dc in first dc, skip next dc, puff (see Special Stitches) in next ch-1 sp, skip next dc, (dc, tr) in last dc. (2 tr, 2 dc & 1 puff)

ROW 3: Ch 4, turn, dc in first tr, skip next dc, (dc, ch 1, dc) in next puff, skip next dc, (dc, tr) in last tr. (2 tr, 4 dc & 1 ch-1 sp)

ROW 4: Ch 4, turn, dc in first tr, skip next dc, 2 dc in sp between next 2 dc, skip next dc, puff in next ch-1 sp, skip next dc, 2 dc in sp between next 2 dc, skip next dc, (dc, tr) in last tr. (2 tr, 6 dc & 1 puff)

ROW 5: Ch 4, turn, dc in first tr, skip next dc, puff in sp between next 2 dc, skip next 2 dc, 4 dc in next puff, skip next 2 dc, puff in sp between next 2 dc, skip next dc, (dc, tr) in last tr. (2 tr, 6 dc & 2 puffs)

ROW 6: Ch 4, turn, dc in first tr, skip next dc, 4 dc in next puff, skip next 2 dc, puff in sp between next 2 dc, skip next 2 dc, 4 dc in next puff, skip next dc, (dc, tr) in last tr. (2 tr, 10 dc & 1 puff)

ROW 7: Ch 4, turn, dc in first tr, skip next dc, [puff in sp between next 2 dc, skip next 2 dc] twice, 4 dc in next puff, [skip next 2 dc, puff in sp between next 2 dc] twice, skip next dc, (dc, tr) in last tr. (2 tr, 6 dc & 4 puffs)

ROW 8: Ch 4, turn, dc in first tr, skip next dc, [4 dc in next puff] across to center, skip next 2 dc, puff in (center) sp between next 2 dc, skip next 2 dc, [4 dc in next puff] across to last 2 sts, skip next dc, (dc, tr) in last tr. (2 tr, 18 dc & 1 puff)

ROW 9: Ch 4, turn, dc in first tr, skip next dc, [puff in sp between next 2 dc, skip next 2 dc] across to center, 4 dc in next (center) puff, [skip next 2 dc, puff in sp between next 2 dc] across to last 2 sts, skip next dc, (dc, tr) in last tr. (2 tr, 6 dc & 6 puffs)

ROWS 10-79 (or to desired size): Rep Rows 8-9, ending on a Puff row (Row 9).

BORDER - optional

Designer's Note: *It's perfectly okay to finish the shawl after Row 79 as it really doesn't need a border. However, I just couldn't get enough of those yummy little puff-stitches and decided to do more in the border!*

ROUND 1: With right side facing (do not turn after last Row), make loop on hook a bit larger and puff in tr last worked, ch 2, working in sides of rows, sc in last row (over post of last tr worked), ch 2, *puff in next row, ch 2, sc in next row, ch 2; rep from * across both sides,

working ([puff, ch 2] twice) in ch at point of shawl, ending with a ([puff, ch 2] twice) in first tr on last row, working across last row, ch 2, sc in first dc, ch 2, working in sps between 2 puff-sts, *puff in next sp, ch 2, sc in next sp; rep from * across, skipping 2 dc, working either puff or sc in sp between center 2 dc, skip next 2 dc (at center of shawl), ending with puff in same last tr, ch 2; join with sl st to first puff. Fasten off.

Designer's Note: *As the puff-st has a locking ch-1, there are actually 3 chs between the puffs and sc-sts (and 2 between the sc and puffs).*

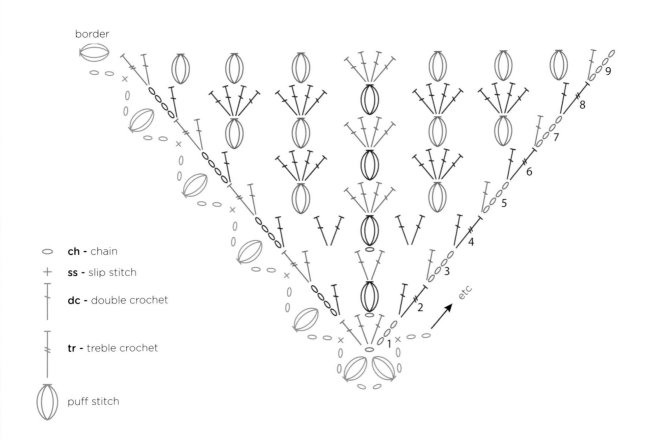

border

ch - chain

ss - slip stitch

dc - double crochet

tr - treble crochet

puff stitch

Puff Scarf And Stroller Blanket "Wendi"

Skill Level
★ ★

As I'm sure you've noticed by now, when it comes to crochet I love playing with stitches, shapes, colors, and yarn. Quite often when I'm in the process of crocheting on one project I come up with all kinds of variations, hence the emergence of this scarf and blanket. It may not look like it, but the "Mechelina Shawl" has the same puff stitches. Using a blue or any other kind of not-so-girly color will make this blanket just as fitting for a baby boy.

Finished Size

Scarf – 13 ½" (34 cm) wide and 80 ½" (204 cm) long

Stroller Blanket - 25 ½" (65 cm) wide and 31 ½" (80 cm) long

WHAT YOU'LL NEED

For Scarf

✻ **DMC Woolly**

Color A (#041) – 2 balls
Color B (#042) – 2 balls
Color C (#043) – 2 balls
Color D (#062) – 2 balls
Color E (#063) – 2 balls
Color F (#065) – 2 balls

For Stroller Blanket

✻ **DMC Woolly**

Main Color – MC (#043) – 8 balls

✻ **DMC Natura Just Cotton**

Contrasting Color - CC (N09) – 1 ball – for Edging

Hook: Size K-10½ (6.5 mm)

Yarn Needle

PATTERN NOTES

✻ Fasten off after each color change

✻ Weave in all ends as you go

✻ Stitch pattern chain multiple = 2+5

SPECIAL STITCHES

Puff Stitch (puff): In same st or sp indicated, [yo hook, insert hook, pull up a loop (to height of hdc)] 4 times (9 loops on hook), yo and draw through all 9 loops on the hook, ch 1 (to lock) (puff stitch made).

Note: *When working in a puff stitch on the following row/round, you insert your hook under the locking chain-stitch.*

PUFF SCARF

ROW 1: (Right Side) With Color A, ch 41, 4 dc in 5th ch from hook, (skipped ch count as ch-1 & first dc), *skip next ch, 4 dc in next ch; rep from * across, ending with skip next ch, dc in last ch. (18 groups of 4-dc & 2 dc)

Designer's Note: *Don't worrry if your piece looks loose and wobbly. This will all be straightened out in the next few rows.*

ROW 2: Ch 3 (counts as first dc, now and throughout), turn, skip next 2 dc, puff (see Special Stitches) in sp between center 2 dc (of 4-dc group), *skip next 4 dc, puff in sp between center 2 dc; rep from * across, ending with skip next 2 dc, dc in last dc. (18 puffs & 2 dc)

Designer's Tip: *If preferred, you can use a ch-2 at the beginning of each new row (instead of the ch-3). I like the slightly straighter sides a ch-2 gives.*

ROW 3: Ch 3, turn, *4 dc in top of next puff; rep from * across, ending with dc in last dc. (18 groups of 4-dc & 2 dc)

ROW 4: Ch 3, turn, skip next 2 dc, puff in sp between center 2 dc (of 4-dc group), *skip next 4 dc, puff in sp between center 2 dc; rep from * across, ending with skip next 2 dc, dc in last dc. (18 puffs & 2 dc)

ROWS 5-28: Rep Rows 3-4. At the end of Row 28, fasten off Color A.

ROW 29: With right side facing, join next Color to first dc, ch 3, *4 dc in top of next puff; rep from * across, ending with dc in last dc. (18 groups of 4-dc & 2 dc)

ROW 30: Rep Row 4.

ROWS 31-56: Rep Rows 3-4. At the end of Row 56, fasten off next Color.

ROWS 57-168: Rep Rows 29-56 four more times, using different colors. At the end of Row 168, fasten off.

STROLLER BLANKET

ROW 1: (Right Side) Using MC, ch 87, 4 dc in 5th ch from hook, (skipped ch count as ch-1 & first dc), *skip next ch, 4 dc in next ch; rep from * across, ending with skip next ch, dc in last ch. (41 groups of 4-dc & 2 dc)

ROW 2: Ch 3 (counts as first dc, now and throughout), turn, skip next 2 dc, puff (see Special Stitches) in sp between center 2 dc (of 4-dc group), *skip next 4 dc, puff in sp between center 2 dc; rep from * across, ending with skip next 2 dc, dc in last dc. (41 puffs & 2 dc)

ROW 3: Ch 3, turn, *4 dc in next puff; rep from * across, ending with dc in last dc. (41 groups of 4-dc & 2 dc)

ROW 4: Ch 3, turn, skip next 2 dc, puff in sp between center 2 dc (of 4-dc group), *skip next 4 dc, puff in sp between center 2 dc; rep from * across, ending with skip next 2 dc, dc in last dc. (41 puffs & 2 dc)

ROWS 5-54: Rep Rows 3-4. At the end of Row 54, fasten off.

BORDER - optional

ROUND 1: Turn, with right side facing, join CC with sl st to first dc, make loop on hook a bit larger and puff in sp before first puff, ch 2, working in sps between 2 puff-sts, *sc in next sp, ch 2, puff in next sp, ch 2; rep from * across, working ([puff, ch 2] 2 times) in sp before last dc; ♥ working in sides of rows, sc in last row (over post of last dc), *ch 2, puff in next row, ch 2, sc in next row; rep from * across ♥, working in sps on other side of starting ch, ([puff, ch 2] 2 times) in first sp, *sc in next sp, ch 2, puff in next sp, ch 2; rep from * across, ending with ([puff, ch 2] 2 times) in last sp; rep from ♥ to ♥ once, (puff, ch 2) once in same sp as first puff; join with sl st to first puff. Fasten off.

Designer's Note: As the puff-st has a locking ch-1, there are actually 3 chs between the puffs and sc-sts (and 2 between the sc and puffs).

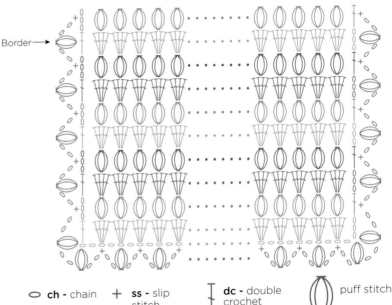

Border →

⬭ **ch** - chain   + **ss** - slip stitch   **dc** - double crochet   ⬭ puff stitch

Ribbed Tartan Cushion

Skill Level
*

If you're in urgent need for a present, or want to give your sofa a quick make-over, crocheting this cushion cover is the ideal solution. This is another one of those "speedy, great-outcome" projects. Don't the surface stitches add just the right touch to this comfy cushion?

Finished Size

To fit about 20" (50 cm)
square pillow form

WHAT YOU'LL NEED

✱ **DMC Natura Just Cotton XL**
Main Color - MC (#06) - 3 balls – for Cushion
For Surface Stitches:
Color A (#03) – 1 ball
Color B (#10) – 1 ball
Color C (#43) – 1 ball

Hook: Size L-11 (8 mm)

Yarn Needle

Pillow Form

Fabric to cover Pillow Form

Needle and matching thread

PATTERN NOTES

✱ Weave in all ends as you go

Designer's Note: If you want to make your cushion a different size, make a 4" (10 cm) square gauge swatch using the pattern stitch. You can then calculate how many stitches and rows you would need to make your custom-sized pillow. Anything's possible as crochet is so versatile!

CUSHION

ROW 1: (Right Side) With MC, ch 44, working in back ridge of chain (see Techniques) sc in 2nd ch from hook, *sc in next ch; rep from * across. (43 sc)

ROW 2: Ch 1, turn, working in back loops (see Techniques) only, sc in each sc across. (43 sc)

Designer's Note: The ribbed pattern is created by crocheting all the sc-stitches in the back loops only of the previous row.

ROWS 3-53: Rep Row 2.

At the end of Row 53, DO NOT fasten off.

SIDE EDGING

With right side facing, work another sc in same last st (to turn the corner), working in sides of rows, sc in each row across, ending with sl st in first ch on starting ch. Fasten off.

With right side facing, join MC with sl st to last ch on starting ch (same as first sc made on Row 1), working in sides of rows, sc in each row across, ending with sl st in first sc on last row. Fasten off.

SURFACE STITCHES

Designer's Note: The rows in which you work the horizontal surface stitches, are 'ditches' formed by the ribbing stitch.

HORIZONTAL ROWS

ROW 1: With right side facing, using Color A, working in Row 15, starting at edge, surface stitch (see Techniques) across row. Fasten off.

ROW 2: Using Color B, repeat Row 1, working in Row 19. Fasten off.

ROW 3: Using Color C, repeat Row 1, working in Row 23. Fasten off.

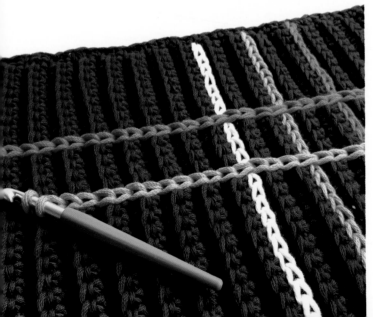

VERTICAL ROWS

ROW 1: With right side facing, using Color A, starting on the second row, at the 11th st on the edge, surface stitch across. Fasten off.

ROW 2: Using Color B, repeat Row 1, starting at the 16th st. Fasten off.

ROW 3: Using Color C, repeat Row 1, starting at the 21st st. Fasten off.

Work your yarn ends to the back of your cushion cover and weave them in.

FINISHING CUSHION

Make a fabric cover for the pillow form. Using needle and thread, sew the Cushion to the front of the cover.

Designer's Note: *I hand-sewed my cushion to a fun tartan fabric cushion cover that had the same colors I used. You could also crochet an identical piece for the back of your cushion.*

Floral Lace Throw
"Heleen"

Skill Level

★ ★

Ever since I started crocheting again, I've been gifted some wonderful vintage magazines - not only knitting and crochet, but other crafts too. A friend's grandmother and my own mother both had quite a collection, and these books and brochures are a true treasure trove. Some of the photos in which garments are modeled actually made me laugh out loud. They look so old-fashioned and very funny in today's terms. Going through these old magazines I've found a few crochet motifs that I really liked. It's been a joy trying to re-create some of them. This throw, "Heleen", consists of one of those vintage motifs - all spiffed up - and I so like how she turned out.

Finished Size

Throw measures about
56 ½" (144 cm) square

Each motif measures 9 ½"
(24 cm)

WHAT YOU'LL NEED

✳ DMC Natura Just Cotton XL
Main Color - MC (Purple #06) - 6 balls
Color A (Ecru #03) – 2 balls
Color B (Fuchsia #43) – 6 balls
Color C (Orange #10) – 4 balls

Hook: Size L-11 (8 mm)

Yarn Needle

PATTERN NOTES

✳ Do not turn after each round

✳ Fasten off after each color change

✳ Weave in all ends as you go

✳ After the First Motif is finished, join the following motifs together on Round 5 to get a grid - 6 motifs wide by 6 motifs long

MOTIF – Make 36

ROUND 1: (Right Side) With Color A, ch 5, join with sl st to first ch to form a ring (or start with a Magic Ring - see Techniques), ch 3 (counts as first dc, now and throughout), 11 dc in ring; join with sl st to first dc (3rd ch of beg ch-3). (12 dc) Fasten off Color A.

ROUND 2: With right side facing, using Color B, join with sc (see Techniques) to any dc, ch 1, *sc in next dc, ch 1; rep from * around; join with sl st to first sc. (12 sc & 12 ch-1 sps)

ROUND 3: Sl st in next ch-1 sp, *ch 14, sl st in same ch-1 sp, sl st in next ch-1 sp; rep from * around; join with sl st to first sl st. (12 ch-14 lps/petals) Fasten off Color B.

ROUND 4: With right side facing, join Color C with sl st to any ch-14 lp, ch 3, (2 dc, ch 3, 3 dc) in same lp (corner made), *[ch 3, sc in next ch-14 lp] twice, ch 3**, (3 dc, ch 3, 3 dc) in next ch-14 lp; rep from * around, ending at ** on final repeat; join with sl st to first dc (3rd ch of beg ch-3). (24 dc, 8 sc & 16 ch-3 sps) Fasten off Color C.

For First Motif Only

ROUND 5: With right side facing, join MC with sl st to any corner ch-3 sp, ch 3, (2 dc, ch 3, 3 dc) in same sp, *ch 3, sc in next sc, ch 3, 3 dc in next ch-3 sp, ch 3, sc in next sc, ch 3**, (3 dc, ch 3, 3 dc) in corner ch-3 sp; rep from * around, ending at ** on final repeat; join with sl st to first dc (3rd ch of beg ch-3). Fasten off MC.

Designer's Note: To keep the lacy look I used both Join-As-You-Go and and PLT (pull loop through) methods for this Throw (see Techniques). You can of course, sew or crochet the motifs together in any way you wish.

- **ss -** slip stitch
- **ch -** chain
- **sc -** single crochet
- **dc -** double crochet

For Remaining Motifs

ROUND 5 (Joining Round): Rep Round 5, but on the side/s that are to be joined, starting at the corner, holding the previous Motif behind (right sides facing), work as follows:

3 dc in corner sp, ch 1, working in previous Motif, sl st in corresponding corner ch-3 sp, ch 1, working in current Motif, 3 dc in same sp, ch 1, working in previous Motif, sl st in corresponding ch-3 sp, ch 1, working in current Motif, sc in next sc, ch 3, make the loop on the hook a bit larger and remove the hook, working in previous Motif, insert the hook from front to back in first dc (of 3-dc group), place loop back on hook and pull through st, working on current motif, dc in corresponding dc, * make the loop on the hook a bit larger and remove the hook, working in previous Motif, insert the hook from front to back in next dc (of 3-dc group), place loop back on hook and pull through st, working on current motif, dc in corresponding dc; rep from * once * once more (all 3 dc-sts joined), ch 3, sc in next sc, ch 1, working on previous motif, sl st in corresponding ch-3 sp, ch 1, working on current motif, 3 dc in corner ch-3 sp, ch 1, working on previous motif, sl st in corresponding corner ch-3 sp, ch 1, working in current motif, 3 dc in same corner ch-3 sp (one side joined) continue with round as established. At the end of the round, fasten off MC.

Designer's Tip: When you attach more than 2 motifs together, at the corner(s) where they all join, sl st into the sl st previously made (the join of the first two Motifs). You can identify this as a little "v" stitch, facing you horizontally.

Striped Baby Blanket "Ingrid"

Skill Level
*

An uncomplicated stitch that gives my crochet a great appearance can make me truly happy. This is exactly what this stitch does. The stitch pattern is a one-row-repeat and makes this project one of those relaxing and meditative jobs. The blanket almost crochets itself! You can make all stripes the same height, or you can play around with the stripes, like I did.

Finished Size

Blanket measures
33 ½" (85 cm) wide by
41" (105 cm) long

WHAT YOU'LL NEED

✻ **DMC Natura Just Cotton Medium**

Color A (#177) – 4 balls
Color B (#31) – 4 balls
Color C (#41) – 3 balls
Color D (#10) – 4 balls
Color E (#444) – 3 balls

Hook: Size K-10½ (6.5 mm)

Yarn Needle

PATTERN NOTES

✻ Fasten off after each color change

✻ Weave in all ends as you go

Designer's Hint on Sizing: You can easily adjust the width of the blanket by increasing/decreasing the number of stitches, as long as you make sure the chains in your foundation row are a multiple of two.

BLANKET

ROW 1: (Right Side) With Color A, ch 112, hdc in 3rd ch from hook, sl st in next ch, *hdc in next ch, sl st in next ch; rep from * across. (110 sts)

ROW 2: Ch 2, turn, hdc in first sl st, sl st in next hdc,*hdc in next sl st, sl st in next hdc; rep from * across.

Designer's Hint: In each new row, the hdc-stitches are always worked in the slip stitches, and the slip stitches are always worked in the hdc-stitches.

ROWS 3-158: Rep Row 2, changing Colors randomly, working an even number of rows with each color change

At the end of Row 158, fasten off and weave in all ends.

Designer's Note: I started off with 8 rows Color A, then 6 rows Color B, followed by 2 rows each of Colors C & D, and then 6 rows of Color E. From there I played it by ear, shuffling the colors and height of the stripes. Have fun with it!

Striped Pouf Cover
"Otto"

This project might look a bit intimidating, but guess what? It's not difficult to make at all! All you need for your pouf cover is a long strip of crochet, that goes all around the side, and two circles - one for the top and one for the bottom. The main thing is to make a swatch before you begin and keep your measuring tape on hand.

My original plan was to crochet a cover and then make and stuff my own custom-sized ottoman to fit the crocheted cover. Then I found a nicely priced, neutral colored pouf and decided to do things the other way around. So I brought the new purchase home and made a custom-fit crochet cover for it. It worked out really well. Happy me! The bottom line is, you can choose which way works best for you.

Finished Size

To fit Ottoman Form
24" (61 cm) diameter and
12" (30.5 cm) high

WHAT YOU'LL NEED

✻ DMC Natura Just Cotton XL

Color A (#42) – 2 balls
Color B (#92) – 2 balls
Color C (#111) – 6 balls
Color D (#12) – 1 ball
Color E (#41) – 1 ball
Color F (#32) – 2 balls
Color G (#73) – 2 balls

Hooks:
Size K-10½ (6.5 mm) – For Top/Bottom & Side Strip
Size J-10 (6 mm) – For Sides Edging

Yarn Needle

PATTERN NOTES

✻ Do not turn after each round (Top/Bottom)

✻ Fasten off after each color change

✻ Weave in all ends as you go

Designer's Notes on Sizing: *Make 4" (10 cm) square swatches, using different sized hooks, keeping in mind that this project needs to be rather firm. When you get the desired fabric, you can calculate how many stitches and rows you'll need for your pouf cover.*

TOP/BOTTOM – Make 2

Designer's Note: *Make as many rounds as you need for your cover, following the established formula.*

ROUND 1: (Right Side) With Color A and larger hook, ch 5, join with sl st to first ch to form a ring (or start with a Magic Ring - see Techniques), ch 3 (counts as first dc, now and throughout), 11 dc in ring; join with sl st to first dc (3rd ch of beg ch-3). (12 dc) Fasten off Color A.

Designer's Note: *Since I'm not a big fan of seeing the ch-3 in every round of a circle, I fastened off at the end of all my rounds (whether I was going to change color or not). Then I rotated my work either 90 or 180 degrees (to prevent diagonal join lines showing) before rejoining with a standing dc. This is just my personal preference.*

ROUND 2: With right side facing, join Color B with sl st to any dc, ch 3, dc in same st as joining, *2 dc in next dc; rep from * around; join with sl st to first dc. (24 dc) Fasten off Color B.

ROUND 3: With right side facing, join Color C with sl st to any dc, ch 3, dc in same st as joining, dc in next dc, *2 dc in next dc, dc in next dc; rep from * around; join with sl st to first dc. (36 dc) Fasten off Color C.

Designer's Note: *Adding 12 additional evenly spaced dc every round keeps the circle round and flat. From here on, each round starts and ends the same; namely starting each round with: joining to any dc, ch 3, and working in the same st as joining (for the first 2 dc) and then working the required number of single dc-sts before the next increase; and ending with join with sl st to first dc. Fasten off at the end of each round. What follows below is the color and stitch pattern formula for each round:*

ROUND 4: With Color D, *2 dc in next dc, dc in each of next 2 dc; rep from * around. (48 dc)

ROUND 5: With Color E, *2 dc in next dc, dc in each of next 3 dc; rep from * around. (60 dc)

ROUND 6: With Color C, *2 dc in next dc, dc in each of next 4 dc; rep from * around. (72 dc)

ROUND 7: With Color C, *2 dc in next dc, dc in each of next 5 dc; rep from * around. (84 dc)

ROUND 8: With Color B, *2 dc in next dc, dc in each of next 6 dc; rep from * around. (96 dc)

ROUND 9: With Color A, *2 dc in next dc, dc in each of next 7 dc; rep from * around. (108 dc)

ROUND 10: With Color F, *2 dc in next dc, dc in each of next 8 dc; rep from * around. (120 dc)

ROUND 11: With Color G, *2 dc in next dc, dc in each of next 9 dc; rep from * around. (132 dc)

ROUND 12: With Color G, *2 dc in next dc, dc in each of next 10 dc; rep from * around. (144 dc)

ROUND 13: With Color C, *2 dc in next dc, dc in each of next 11 dc; rep from * around. (156 dc)

ROUND 14: With Color B, *2 dc in next dc, dc in each of next 12 dc; rep from * around. (168 dc)

ROUND 15: With Color C, *2 dc in next dc, dc in each of next 13 dc; rep from * around. (180 dc)

Designer's Hint: *End your circle rounds with the same color you want to use to sew your strip to the rounds.*

SIDE STRIP

Designer's Note: *Based on your gauge swatch, you will need to determine how many chain stitches you need to get the height of your pouf. In my case, I needed 31 dc per row.*

ROW 1: With color of choice and larger hook, ch 33, working in the back ridge of chain (see Techniques), dc in 4th ch from hook (skipped ch count as first dc), *dc in next ch; rep from * across. (31 dc)

Designer's Tip: *If preferred, you can use a ch-2 at the beginning of each new row (instead of the ch-3). I like the slightly straighter sides a ch-2 gives.*

ROW 2: Ch 3, turn, *dc in next dc; rep from * across. (31 dc)

Designer's Note: *When changing colors, fasten off previous color at the end of the row. Start next row with: Turn, join next Color with sl st to first dc, ch 3, and continue from * in Row 2.*

ROWS 3-92 (or to desired length): Rep Row 2, using colors of your choice.

Designer's Note: *I did not plan my colors, nor the height of my stripes in advance. I just chose them as I went along. I made sure to begin and end my strip with the same color, so my seam would blend in; I used dark brown (Color C). Here is my final color change list:*

ROWS 1 - 6: Color C	**ROWS 57 - 58:** Color F
ROWS 7 - 8: Color G	**ROWS 59 - 60:** Color E
ROWS 9 - 11: Color E	**ROW 61:** Color B
ROWS 12 - 13: Color F	**ROW 62:** Color C
ROWS 14 - 19: Color B	**ROW 63:** Color D
ROWS 20 - 22: Color A	**ROW 64:** Color A
ROWS 23 - 24: Color C	**ROW 65:** Color G
ROWS 25: Color D	**ROW 66:** Color F
ROWS 26: Color C	**ROW 67:** Color C
ROWS 27: Color D	**ROW 68:** Color B
ROWS 28: Color C	**ROW 69:** Color F
ROWS 29: Color D	**ROW 70:** Color C
ROWS 30 - 32: Color C	**ROW 71:** Color E
ROW 33: Color B	**ROWS 72 - 76:** Color C
ROW 34: Color E	**ROWS 77 - 78:** Color G
ROW 35: Color A	**ROWS 79 - 81:** Color E
ROW 36: Color G	**ROWS 82 - 83:** Color F
ROW 37: Color C	**ROWS 84 - 85:** Color A
ROWS 38 - 41: Color F	**ROW 86:** Color C
ROWS 42 - 45: Color B	**ROWS 87 - 88:** Color B
ROWS 46 - 49: Color A	**ROW 89:** Color C
ROWS 50 - 53: Color C	**ROWS 90 -91:** Color G
ROWS 54 - 56: Color G	**ROW 92:** Color C

JOINING THE SIDE STRIP

Sew in all ends before continuing.

Designer's Note: *Given all the color changes there were a lot (a lot!) of ends to sew in. If that's something you don't like, you might want to consider making fewer stripes, or even crochet your cover in one color. That could also look pretty!*

With right sides facing, join the last row to the starting chain, to form a cylinder (to fit around the pouf).

Designer's Note: *I used the flat Zipper Join (see Techniques) for this, but any sewn or crocheted join is fine.*

SIDES EDGING

ROUND 1: With right side facing, using Color C and smaller hook, working in sides of rows, join with sc (see Techniques) to any row, sc in same row, evenly work 2 sc in each row around, working 1 sc in joining; join with sl st to first sc. (185 sc) Fasten off.

Rep Round 1 on other side, making sure you get the same number of stitches as on the first side. Fasten off.

FINISHING THE COVER

Now you need to join your Top and Bottom circles to your joined Side Strip.

Designer's Note: *I again used the flat Zipper Join here, but sewing or crocheting the pouf together is perfect as well.*

With right sides facing, using Color C, join Top to edge of Side Strip cylinder. To make sure they fit together, you might need to do some decreases. Fasten off.

Designer's Hint: *In my case, I had 180 sts in the last round of my circles, and I had 185 sc around each end of the cylinder, so I knew I needed to decrease 5 sts on each end of the Side Strip. When joining the pieces together, I decreased by 1 stitch every 36 stitches for my pieces to fit. (See Techniques for decreasing using Zipper Join).*

Insert pouf before repeating the joining with the Bottom to Side Strip cylinder (including the decreasing, if used). Fasten off.

You're all done! Now sit down, have a drink and put your feet up (on your pouf)!

Sunshine Blanket "Quinn"

Skill Level
**

Designing and crocheting this blanket was such a joy. The wonderfully soft yarn, the happy-making color, and only needing thirty-six rather large squares to make a nicely sized blanket... My kind of project! Here's how you create your own comfortable piece of sunshine.

Finished Size

Blanket measures about
43" (110 cm) square

Each motif measures 7"
(18 cm) square

WHAT YOU'LL NEED

✱ **DMC Natura Just Cotton Medium**
Main Color - MC (#09 Mirabelle) - 20 balls

Hooks:
Size K-10½ (6.5 mm) - for Motifs
Size J-10 (6 mm) - for Border

Yarn Needle

PATTERN NOTES

✱ Do not turn after each round

✱ Weave in all ends as you go

SPECIAL STITCHES

Beginning Popcorn (beg-pc): Ch 3, 2 dc in st or sp indicated, drop loop from hook, insert hook from front to back through 3rd ch (of ch-3), place dropped loop on hook and pull through st (first popcorn made).

Popcorn (pc): Work 3 dc in st or sp indicated, drop loop from hook, insert hook from front to back through first dc (of 3-dc group), place dropped loop on hook and pull through st (popcorn made).

- • **ss -** slip stitch
- ◯ **ch -** chain
- │ **dc -** double crochet
- ⬭ 3-dc popcorn

MOTIF – Make 36

ROUND 1: (Right Side) With MC and larger hook, ch 10, join with sl st to first ch to form ring; beg-pc (see Special Stitches above) in ring, ch 3, pc (see Special Stitches) in ring, *ch 1, 3 dc in ring, ch 1, (pc, ch 3, pc) in ring; rep from * twice more, ch 1, 3 dc in ring, ch 1; join with sl st to first ch-3 sp. (8 popcorns, 12 dc, 8 ch-1 sps & 4 corner ch-3 sps)

ROUND 2: (Beg-pc, ch 3, pc) in same ch-3 sp, *ch 1, 2 dc in next dc, dc in next dc, 2 dc in last dc, ch 1**, (pc, ch 3, pc) in next ch-3 sp; rep from * around, ending at ** on final repeat; join with sl st to first ch-3 sp. (8 popcorns, 20 dc, 8 ch-1 sps & 4 corner ch-3 sps)

ROUNDS 3-5: (Beg-pc, ch 3, pc) in same ch-3 sp, *ch 1, 2 dc in next dc, [dc in next dc] across to last dc, 2 dc in last dc, ch 1**, (pc, ch 3, pc) in next ch-3 sp; rep from * around, ending at ** on final repeat; join with sl st to first ch-3 sp.

At the end of Round 5, there are 8 popcorns, 44 dc, 8 ch-1 sps & 4 corner ch-3 sps. Fasten off.

ASSEMBLY OF MOTIFS

The 36 motifs are assembled in a 6 motif by 6 motif grid.

Designer's Note: *If you are joining the motifs as you go, after the first motif, use Round 5 as the joining Round for the rest of the Motifs. Of course, you can make 36 complete motifs (Rounds 1-5), and then either sew or crochet them together. My preference is the "PLT (pull loop through) Join-as-you-go" method (see Crochet Techniques), as follows:*

ROUND 5 (Joining Round): Rep Round 5, but on the side/s that are to be joined, starting at the corner, holding the previous Motif behind (right sides facing), work as follows:

Pc in corner ch-3 sp, ch 1, working in previous Motif, sl st in corresponding corner ch-3 sp, ch 1, working in current Motif, pc in same corner ch-3 sp, ch 1, make the loop on the hook a bit larger and remove the hook, working in previous Motif, insert the hook from front to back in corresponding first dc, place loop back on hook and pull through st, working on current motif, dc in next dc, remove hook from loop, and working in previous Motif, insert the hook in next dc, place loop back on hook and pull through st, working on current motif, dc in same dc, *working in previous Motif, insert the hook in next dc, place loop back on hook and pull through st, working on current Motif, dc in next dc; rep from * across, remembering to work 2 dc in last dc of current Motif, ch 1, pc in corner ch-3 sp, ch 1, working in previous Motif, sl st in corresponding corner ch-3 sp, ch 1, working in current Motif, pc in same corner ch-3 sp; continue with Round 5 as established. Fasten off.

Designer's Tip: *When you attach more than 2 motifs together, at the corner(s) where they all join, sl st into the sl st previously made (the join of the first two Motifs). You can identify this as a little "v" stitch, facing you horizontally.*

BORDER

ROUND 1: With right side of completed Blanket facing, using smaller hook, join with sl st to any st, ch 1, crab stitch (see Techniques) in each st or sp around, working 2 crab sts in each corner; join with sl st to first sc. Fasten off. Lightly steam block blanket before use.

Crochet Basics & Techniques

Crochet Basics

SLIP KNOT

Almost every crochet project starts with a slip knot on the hook. This is not mentioned in any pattern – it is assumed.

To make a slip knot, form a loop with your yarn (the tail end hanging behind your loop); insert the hook through the loop, and pick up the ball end of the yarn. Draw yarn through loop. Keeping loop on hook, gently tug the tail end to tighten the knot. Tugging the ball end tightens the loop.

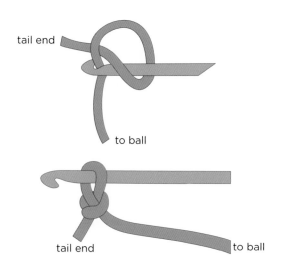

YARN OVER (yo)

This is a common practice, especially with the taller stitches.

With a loop on your hook, wrap the yarn (attached to the ball) from back to front around the shaft of your hook.

CHAIN STITCH (ch)

The chain stitch is the foundation of most crochet projects.

The foundation chain is a series of chain stitches in which you work the first row of stitches.

To make a chain stitch, you start with a slip knot (or loop) on the hook. Yarn over and pull the yarn through the loop on your hook (first chain stitch made). For more chain stitches, repeat: Yarn over, pull through loop on hook.

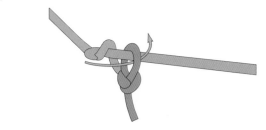

Hint: Don't pull the stitches too tight, otherwise they will be difficult to work in.

When counting chain stitches, do not count the slip knot, nor the loop on the hook. Only count the number of 'v's.

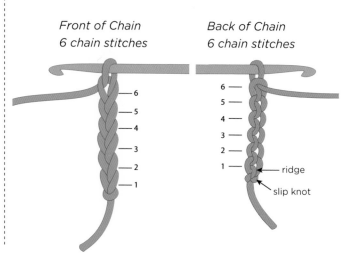

Front of Chain
6 chain stitches

Back of Chain
6 chain stitches

SLIP STITCH (sl st)

Starting with a loop on your hook, insert hook in stitch or space specified and pull up a loop, pulling it through the loop on your hook as well.
The slip stitch is commonly used to attach new yarn and to join rounds.

Attaching a New Color or New Ball of Yarn (or Joining with a Slip Stitch (join with sl st)).
Make a slip knot with the new color (or yarn) and place loop on hook. Insert hook from front to back in the (usually) first stitch (unless specified otherwise). Yarn over and pull loop through stitch and loop on hook (slip stitch made).

SINGLE CROCHET (sc)

Starting with a loop on your hook, insert hook in stitch or space specified and draw up a loop (two loops on hook). Yarn over and pull yarn through both the loops on your hook (first sc made).

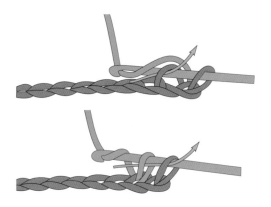

The height of a single crochet stitch is one chain high.

When working single crochet stitches into a foundation chain, begin the first single crochet in the second chain from the hook. The skipped chain stitch provides the height of the stitch.

At the beginning of a single crochet row or round, start by making one chain stitch (to get the height) and work the first single crochet stitch into first stitch (Note: The one chain stitch is never counted as a single crochet stitch).

HALF-DOUBLE CROCHET (hdc)

Starting with a loop on your hook, yarn over hook before inserting hook in stitch or space specified and draw up a loop (three loops on hook). Yarn over and pull yarn through all three loops (first hdc made).

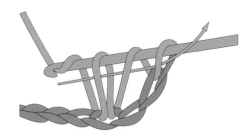

The height of a half-double crochet stitch is two chains high.
When working half-double crochet stitches into a foundation chain, begin the first stitch in the third chain from the hook. The two skipped chains provide the height. When starting a row or round with a half-double crochet stitch, make two chain stitches and work in the first stitch (Note: The two chain stitches are never counted as a half-double stitch).

DOUBLE CROCHET (dc)

Starting with a loop on your hook, yarn over hook before inserting hook in stitch or space specified and draw up a loop (three loops on hook). Yarn over and pull yarn through two loops (two loops remain on hook). Yarn over and pull yarn through remaining two loops on hook (first dc made).

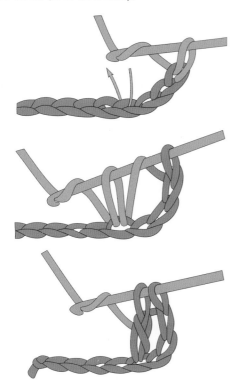

The height of a double crochet stitch is three chains high.

When working double crochet stitches into a foundation chain, begin the first stitch in the fourth chain from the hook.

The three skipped chains count as the first double crochet stitch. When starting a row or round with a double crochet stitch, make three chain stitches (which count as the first double crochet), skip the first stitch (under the chains) and work a double crochet in the next (second) stitch. On the following row or round, when you work in the 'made' stitch, you will be working in the top chain (3rd chain stitch of the three chains).

TREBLE (OR TRIPLE) CROCHET (tr)

Starting with a loop on your hook, yarn over hook twice before inserting hook in stitch or space specified and draw up a loop (four loops on hook). Yarn over and pull yarn through two loops (three loops remain on hook). Again, make a yarn over and pull yarn through two loops (two loops remain on hook). Once more, yarn over and pull through remaining two loops (first tr made).

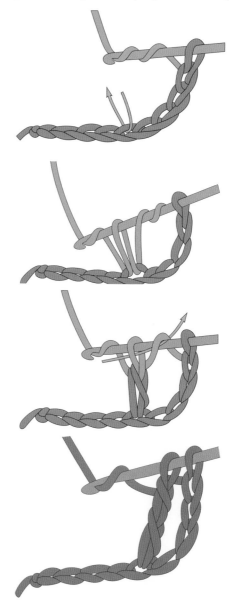

The height of a treble crochet stitch is four chains high.

When working treble crochet stitches into a foundation chain, begin the first stitch in the fifth chain from the hook. The four skipped chains count as the first treble crochet stitch. When starting a row or round with a treble crochet stitch, make four chain stitches (which count as the first treble crochet), skip the first stitch (under the chains) and work a treble crochet in the next (second) stitch. On the following row or round, when you work in the 'made' stitch, you will be working in the top chain (4th chain stitch of the four chains).

DOUBLE TREBLE (OR DOUBLE TRIPLE) CROCHET (dtr)

Starting with a loop on your hook, yarn over hook three times before inserting hook in stitch or space specified and draw up a loop (five loops on hook). *Yarn over and pull yarn through two loops; rep from * three times more (until only the loop on your hook remains (first dtr made).

The height of a double treble crochet stitch is five chains high.

HEIGHT OF CHAIN STITCHES

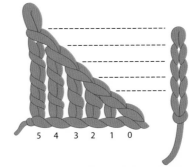

5 Double Treble Crochet
4 Treble Crochet
3 Double Crochet
2 Half-Double Crochet
1 Single Crochet
0 Slip Stitch

Crochet Techniques

MAGIC RING

Instead of starting with a ring consisting of a number of chain stitches, one can use a Magic Ring.

You start as if you were making a slip knot: Form a loop with your yarn (the tail end hanging behind your loop); insert the hook through the loop, and pick up the ball end of the yarn. Draw yarn through loop. Here is where things change... Do not tighten up the knot or loop. Make a chain stitch (to 'lock' the ring), then continue with the 'height' chain stitches. Work the required stitches into the ring (over the tail strand). When all the stitches are done, gently tug the tail end to close the ring, before joining the round (if specified). Remember, make sure this tail is firmly secured when weaving in the end.

STANDING STITCHES

Standing stitches replace the normal "join a new color (or yarn) with a slip stitch to the stitch or space specified and then chain up to the stitch height". They are made by working the stitch from the top-down.

Single Crochet Stitch Standing Stitch (join with sc)

With slip knot on hook, insert hook into stitch or space indicated and pull up a loop (two loops on hook). Yarn over and pull through both loops on hook (first single crochet made).

Half-Double Crochet Standing Stitch

With slip knot on hook, yarn over, (holding the two loops with thumb) insert hook into stitch or space indicated and pull up a loop (three loops on hook). Yarn over and pull through all three loops (standing half-double crochet made).

Double Crochet Standing Stitch

With slip knot on hook, yarn over, (holding the two loops with thumb) insert hook into stitch or space indicated and pull up a loop (three loops on hook). Yarn over and pull through two loop (two loops on hook). Yarn over and pull through remaining two loops (standing double crochet made).

CHANGING COLORS / ATTACHING NEW YARN

Changing to a new ball of yarn or a new color, ideally should happen when starting a new row or round.

Instead of fastening off one color and then joining a new color with a slip stitch or Standing Stitch, one can use the following technique:

In the stitch before the change, work up to last step of the stitch (In most cases the last step of a stitch is the final "yarn over, pull through remaining stitches on hook"). This is where the change happens. Here you will use the new color in the "yarn over" and pull it through the remaining stitches.

This technique is not only used for color changing. It can also be used to introduce a new ball of yarn (of the same color) while working on a project.

BACK RIDGE OF FOUNDATION CHAIN

Most projects start with a foundation chain – a string of chain stitches. One can identify the front of the chain stitches by seeing 'v's. When you turn the foundation chain over, at the back are a string of 'bumps'. This is referred to as the back ridge (or back bar) of the chain.

When working in the back ridge of the chain stitches, one inserts the hook from front to back through the 'bar' (the 'v' is underneath the hook) and pulls the yarn through the 'bar'.

Working your first row in the back ridge of the foundation chain, gives a neat finish to your project. If you are seaming pieces together, it also creates a flatter seam.

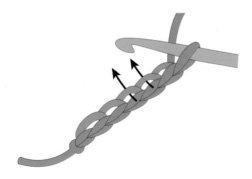

FRONT AND BACK LOOPS

Each stitch has what we call 'v's on the top. Unless otherwise specified, all stitches are worked by inserting the hook under both the loops – under the 'v'.

Sometimes a pattern calls for stitches worked in either the front or back loops. These are the two loops that make up the 'v'. The front loops are the loops closest to you and the back loops are the loops furthest from you. Working in the front or back loops only, creates a decorative ridge (of the unworked loops).

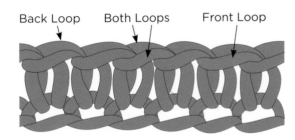

Back Loop   Both Loops   Front Loop

THIRD LOOPS

Besides the Back and Front Loops of any basic stitch, there is also a 'third loop'. This loop looks like a horizontal bar and is found at the back of the stitch. When the 'v's of the stitches are facing you, it is found behind the back loop. When the 'v's are facing away from you, it is the loop below the front loop. Working stitches into the third loop, creates a decorative line of 'v's.

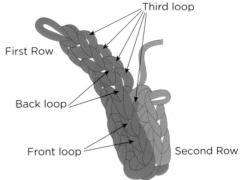

Third loop

First Row

Back loop

Front loop   Second Row

CRAB STITCH

This stitch is also known as Reverse Single Crochet (rev-sc) and creates a neat edging to a project. It is similar to the regular single crochet stitch but is worked in the opposite direction – left to right (for right-handers) and right to left (for left-handers).

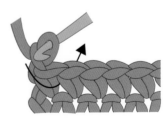

With a loop on the hook, * insert hook in next st to the right (or left for left-handers) and pull up loop, yarn over and pull through both loops on hook. Repeat from * across (or around).

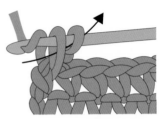

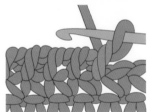

SURFACE STITCHES

These decorative stiches look like embroidered chain stitches.

Make a slip knot. Insert hook as specified in pattern from front (right side) to back (wrong side) of fabric. Place slip knot on hook (at back). Keeping the yarn to the back, pull the loop of the slip knot through to the front (keeping the knot at the back). *Insert hook in next spot specified (from front to back), pull up yarn through fabric and through loop on hook (slip stitch). Repeat from * as per pattern.

JOINING SEAMS

There are many ways ways to join your crochet pieces together. Once all your crocheted motifs or pieces are finished, you can choose to:

1) Sew them together, using needle and yarn, matching stitches and rows where possible. There are various sewing stitches you can use, the most common one being the whip-stitch.

2) Crochet the seams together, using either a slip stitch or a row of single crochet stitches. These can be worked from the wrong side or can be used decoratively on the right side of the fabric. Another crocheted seam is the flat 'Zipper Join' (see below).

3) A third method, "join-as-you-go", is what it says. While you're crocheting on one piece, you're joining it to an already finished piece. Generally, the join is a slip stitch worked into a chain space on the finished piece. When there are no chain spaces available, another technique is PLT – "pull loop through" (see below).

Zipper Join

This join is worked on the right side of the fabric and the chain created by the slip stitches lies flat in the 'ditch' between the front loops of both pieces.
With both pieces of fabric lying side by side –

right sides facing, *insert hook from front to back through back loop on the first and then repeat in the corresponding stitch on the other piece, yarn over and pull yarn through both stitches and the loop on hook (slip stitch made). Repeat from * across.
Whenever you come to an intersection of another seam, make a chain stitch and skip the seam. Continue with the zipper join on the other side of the seam.

When you need to decrease stitches while working the zipper join, on the side that needs decreasing, you insert hook from front to back through each of the next two stitches. The yarn is then pulled through three stitches (one single stitch on one side and two stitches on the decrease side) together with the loop on hook.

PLT Pull LoopThrough

Working with both pieces right sides facing, on the current piece, make the loop on hook slightly larger and remove the hook. Insert hook from front to back through the corresponding stitch on the finished piece and pick up the loop and pull it through the stitch. Then continue working in the current piece until you need to join again.

BLOCKING

To give your crochet creations a beautiful and professional look, it is advisable to block them all when finished. You can also block motifs before joining them together.

Wet-blocking is done by pinning out your piece to size and shape (using non-rust pins) on a clean, flat and soft surface. You can use towels, foam board, or rubber mat tiles.

Depending on the yarn you used, you can gently wash your crochet pieces first and then pin them out, or you can pin out the dry pieces, and lightly spritz them with water, or (if they are NOT acrylic) hover a steam iron over them. Never let the iron touch the crochet pieces. Leave the pinned pieces to dry completely.

Thank you

I'm sure it did not go unnoticed that a lot of the crochet projects in this book carry women's names. It's my way to honor the women that have played, and still play an important role in my life and creative journey.

It is with a heart full of gratitude that I write these words. Making this book has been an incredible adventure. I would not have been able to do it - and enjoy it as much as I did - without the help I received from so many wonderful and lovely people.

Of course, it all started with an email from my fantastic publisher, Tuva Publishing. Thank you, Kader and Ayhan, for giving me this really great opportunity, for your trust, confidence, and creative freedom, offering support when needed. It's been a joy working with you and your entire team. I'm also greatly indebted to my fantastic crochet tech editor, Wendi Cusins. Even though literally oceans apart, we were always on the same page when it came to the book. Thank you, Wendi, I loved our teamwork.

No yarn - no projects. So, a huge thank you goes out to DMC and G. Brouwer & Zn for providing the beautiful yarn I had available to me. A special thank you to Remco Brouwer for always going the extra mile.

I'm immensely thankful for the fabulous women that formed my team of testers. When I asked them to step aboard, I kind of jokingly called them the "Terrific Testers", and this is precisely what they turned out to be. They all did an awesome job. Besides all the crocheting, testing and re-testing of my patterns, they were there for me during this whole exciting journey, offering help in many other ways and always cheering me on. I loved our TT-meetings, when we enjoyed each other's company, crocheting (what else), eating, laughing... It's been wonderful getting to learn more about the four of you. This thank you comes from the bottom of my heart and goes "to infinity and beyond" - dearest Heleen Scharstuhl, Inez de Goede, Ingrid Danvers and Lotte van Dinteren!

And then there's my CraftKitchen colleagues and friends: many thanks to Janneke Assink for your support and for extra test-driving two of the patterns, and to both Lisanne Multem and Janneke for the fab photos taken during our very first and oh-so-fun photo-shoot.

The second photo-shoot was equally enjoyable: big thanks to sweet Sem for being the loveliest and best nine-year old model ever!

Thank you, Joyce van de Kerkhof, for so generously allowing me to use your marvelous "www.mez11.nl"-labels. I love how they've put the perfect finishing touch on my projects.

A heartfelt thank you also goes out to my extended family and close friends for their support during these past months.

The photography in this book is mostly a family affair. Some of the photos were taken in my brothers' apartment - thank you Lex & Marcel. A lot of the pics were shot by our two talented kids as my dedicated photographers, and I so love that. It was a true pleasure to step out of the parent-child role and actually work together with Quinn and Carter.

This brings me to the delightful people that deserve my last, enormous "thank you", my loving and supportive family: Lex, Quinn and Carter - you're the very best. As always, your encouragement, faith, warm blanket of love, the feeling you're proud of me, your hands-on help and patience, were and are priceless. I honestly could not have done this without you: Team Dekkers rules!

Love,
Marianne xx